Praise for
*The Dream of You*

"My friend Jo has a pastor's heart, and that heart shines through every page of this beautiful book. Reading these pages is like learning from a wise friend."
　—SHAUNA NIEQUIST, *New York Times* best-selling author
　　of *Present Over Perfect*

"In these pages, Jo's trademark wisdom is on display and accessible to everyone who settles in for the ride. Through her gift of delivering essential messaging with wit and wonder, Jo rekindles the desires of your heart and reintroduces you to the life you were meant to live. If you and this book have found your way to each other, I have just two words to share: lucky you!"
　—DEIDRA RIGGS, national speaker and author of *One: Unity in a Divided World*

"We live in a noisy culture. It feels as if nearly everyone is screaming about who we ought to be, creating a heightened sense of anxiety and confusion. Jo Saxton, in *The Dream of You*, speaks prophetically, pastorally, and practically to this crisis of identity, because if our identity is not in Christ, we'll struggle with deep insecurity. We'll pursue everything, trying to fill our lives with meaning. With her own personal vulnerability, Jo invites us to relinquish our broken identities and return once more to the One who created us."
　—REV. EUGENE CHO, senior pastor, Quest Church, and author of *Overrated: Are We More in Love with the Idea of Changing the World Than Actually Changing the World?*

"The thing I admire most about the words Jo writes is the way in which she lives them. She carries this message like a jug and passes out cups of cool water to those who have been running faster, harder, and longer. If you have lost sight of where you are going, *The Dream of You* is a guidebook to help you get back on track."
　—BIANCA JUAREZ OLTHOFF, speaker, advocate, and best-selling author of *Play with Fire*

"Jo is a friend of ours. She's a lot of fun, but she's also filled to the brim with guts and grit and Jesus. This isn't a book about Jo; it's about leaving behind who you thought you were and becoming who God made you to be. You'll be captivated by her stories and swept away by God's love."

—MARIA AND BOB GOFF, authors and Jo's friends

"Who do you see when you look in the mirror or take a selfie? Maybe you see blemishes, pudgy cheeks, imperfection, emptiness, and a lost identity of yourself. *The Dream of You* is a reality check for many who have gotten lost in what society requires and what others desire of you. These false identities have created a sunken silo, sometimes unrecognizable to us. Jo brilliantly calls us to remember our true identities, discovering the people God created us to be. Jo takes us on a personal discovery of ourselves, interwoven through personal and biblical stories of broken identity that keep us from living the lives we were created to live. She invites you to be brave, bold, and courageous, whether you were told you had to work harder than everyone else or that you're not good enough and will never be enough. God wants to redeem our stories and capture our hearts. God wants to restore your name and purpose. He wants you to embrace His redeeming love."

—LATASHA MORRISON, founder and president of Be the Bridge

"Absolutely hands down, Jo is one of my most trusted voices in Christian leadership. When she teaches us about our identity in Christ, being deeply known and loved and purposed by God in *The Dream of You,* the greatest testament I can offer toward her credibility is that she texts me some version of that message every single week. She leads auditoriums full of people, and she leads me one-on-one. She is the real deal, and every word of this book is the gospel truth."

—JEN HATMAKER, *New York Times* best-selling author of
 *Of Mess and Moxie*

"In *The Dream of You,* Jo Saxton takes her readers by the hand as she walks us through the many broken identities she once claimed and has now relinquished in order to retain the only One who is necessary. She does so by inviting us into the most painful touchpoints in her life while describing what it has meant for her to navigate her intersectional identities as a black woman who is the daughter of Nigerian immigrants. External voices scream incessantly, telling us who we ought to be. Even heroines like Wonder Woman become cruel taskmasters whose images reminds us that we will never measure up. Jo Saxton calls us to give up the ever-elusive chase to be everything but what God has called us to be and we are all the better for it."

—EKEMINI UWAN, public theologian

"Henri Nouwen wrote, 'One of the great tragedies of our life is that we keep forgetting who we are.' Jo Saxton's *The Dream of You* carries the antidote to this universal problem—a book that calls us to remember who we really are. It is a primal, human book, crackling with life and wind and Spirit. *The Dream of You* doesn't just speak *about* our shared human condition, but *into* it with revelatory clarity, like the prophet Ezekiel speaking to the valley of dry bones. To truly hear these words is for your soul to come to life. The dream Jo Saxton writes about will actually be your awakening."

—JONATHAN MARTIN, author of *How to Survive a Shipwreck* and *Prototype*

"Jo writes like she teaches. With a deeply rooted foundation in Scripture, Jo fills the pages of *The Dream of You* with biblical meat along with challenging, grace-filled application. Most of this beautiful balance of truth and grace unfolds in her personal, and sometimes painful, journey. Authentic, funny, relatable, poignant, and tender, this book is packed with practical direction for each of us to discover and embrace our true identity in the unchanging character of God. I am excited for how lives will be impacted as a result of reading the truths found in the pages of this wonderful book."

—VIVIAN MABUNI, speaker and author of *Warrior in Pink: A Story of Cancer, Community, and the God Who Comforts*

"Jo writes with the same gusto with which she speaks, from a life lived fiercely and faithfully. Without an understanding of our core identity, we will squander the short time we have here on earth and miss out on the story the God of the universe has written for each of us, one of meaning and intimacy. Jo challenges us to live as we were meant to, with power and purpose."

—JENNIE ALLEN, author of *Nothing to Prove*; founder and visionary of the IF:Gathering

"In reading Jo's book, I wondered if she had been reading my journals or eavesdropping on my conversations. Her writing finds us where we are, whether we are broken, surviving, healing, or desperate for a change. This book is not only Jo's letter to her readers, but it is a great reminder of the letter God is writing to all of us. Let this book serve as your loving wake-up call to God's dream of you."

—AMENA BROWN, spoken word poet and author of *How to Fix a Broken Record*

"Jo Saxton didn't just give us a book. She gave us an invitation to dig into Scripture, to listen to her journey, and to be honest with ourselves and with God. She walks us through her story as a Nigerian Brit now in the US. You can almost hear her laugh and sip her tea as she tells us about her childhood hurts and dreams, and she weaves it all together with a reminder that God sees us and knows our dreams. What a needed reminder!"

—KATHY KHANG, author of the forthcoming book *Raise Your Voice* and coauthor of *More Than Serving Tea*

"Careful. You're about to have an encounter with Jo Saxton here in this book, and life may never be the same! Every time I am with Jo, I am challenged, refocused, inspired, and a bit more free to rise to my full capacity as a woman of God. With her trademark boldness and authenticity, Jo will empower you, embolden you, and send you out with purpose and hope to become who God always intended for you to be all along."

—SARAH BESSEY, author of *Jesus Feminist* and *Out of Sorts*

# THE
# DREAM
## OF
# YOU

**LET GO OF BROKEN IDENTITIES
AND LIVE THE LIFE YOU WERE MADE FOR**

# JO SAXTON

**WATERBROOK**

THE DREAM OF YOU

Details and names in some anecdotes and stories have been changed to protect the identities of the persons involved.

Trade Paperback ISBN 978-0-7352-8982-6
eBook ISBN 978-0-7352-8983-3

Cover design by Kelly L. Howard

Published in the United States by WaterBrook, an imprint of the Crown Publishing Group, a division of Penguin Random House LLC, New York.

WATERBROOK® and its deer colophon are registered trademarks of Penguin Random House LLC.

Library of Congress Cataloging-in-Publication Data
Names: Saxton, Jo, 1974– author.
Title: The dream of you : let go of broken identities and live the life you were made for / Jo Saxton.
Description: First Edition. | Colorado Springs : WaterBrook, 2018. | Includes bibliographical references.
Identifiers: LCCN 2017035581| ISBN 9780735289826 (pbk.) | ISBN 9780735289833 (electronic)
Subjects: LCSH: Christian women—Religious life. | Identity (Psychology)—Religious aspects—Christianity. | Women—Religious aspects—Christianity.
Classification: LCC BV4527 .S263 2018 | DDC 248.8/43—dc23 LC record available at https://lccn.loc.gov/2017035581

Printed in the United States of America
2019

10  9  8  7  6  5  4

SPECIAL SALES
Most WaterBrook books are available at special quantity discounts when purchased in bulk by corporations, organizations, and special-interest groups. Custom imprinting or excerpting can also be done to fit special needs. For information, please e-mail specialmarketscms@penguinrandomhouse.com or call 1-800-603-7051.

*To all the wonderful women I meet*
*at conferences, churches, over coaching calls and coffee.*
*You're amazing.*
*Yes, you!*
*with love, Jo*

# Contents

# Foreword

There's a brilliant family of people in Africa, called the Himba. When a Himba woman is expecting a child, she goes out into the wilderness with a few of her sisters, and together they wait till they hear in their hearts the song of the coming child.

Himba women wait as long as they need to; they wait under stars; they wait until the dream of the child begins to beat like a singular rhythm under their hearts. Because these sisters know that every heart has its own unique beat—its own wild and blazing purpose. And when the Himba women attune to the song of the coming child, they circle around and together they sing the miraculous refrain of the expected child.

Then they return to the gathering of their people and teach this child's unique song to the waiting community.

When the anticipated child is finally born and taken into arms, the Himba family enfolds her with their presence, and their voices rise, singing the child's own song to her breathing in first air of this earth.

Later, when the child begins her schooling, the villagers gather and boldly chant the child's song. And then when the child passes through the initiation to adulthood, the Himba again circle round and sing hopefully and bravely. At the time of marriage, the young woman again hears the assuring notes of her very own song, carrying her forward to meet her hopes.

But there is one more occasion upon which the Himba sing.

If at any time during her life the sister loses her way, falls short, forgets who she really is, or lets anything steal the dream of who she is meant to be, she is gently beckoned to the center of the village. And there she stands, her people forming a safe, ringing circle around her, like her own galaxy of stars.

Then the villagers sing, letting the beat of her drum, the rhythm of her own being rouse her to wake to the dream of her soul again. They sing her own soul song to her because Himba sisters believe that change happens most when we remember who we are and whose we are.

This is what every woman must know: the first tactic of the Enemy is always to distort your identity. Genuine serenity is found only when you know your genuine identity. And you can find your true destiny only when you find your true identity.

Do you know who you really are under the false facades and the piles of work and the relentless exhaustion and the suffocating masks?

Maybe for too long you can't seem to wake from the nightmare of feeling like "not enough"—not good enough, smart enough, pretty enough, trendy enough, accomplished enough—and this is what keeps you from waking to the abundantly more than enough God has for you.

Maybe your heart has thickened into this long, scarred callus, and you've numbed yourself to getting wounded ever again. You smile, you laugh, you nod—but when you look in the mirror, you can't even remember who you really are or who you were bravely meant to be. But these pages you hold in your hand are your song sheets to wake you to "the dream of you."

These pages will sing your beauty when you see yourself ugly.

This symphony will sing your worth when you see yourself worn out.

These lyrics will sing hope when you feel deeply hurt.

This song will sing of you as His Beloved when you struggle to believe.

Your uncommonly wise sister, Jo Saxton, intimately knows the song of you because she listens in rare and luminous ways to the heartbeat of your Father. She has written a symphony for your soul, a movement of song that will find you and remind you, because you are not defined by the blind or the unkind or mankind, but only by the Conductor of the Cosmos who sang the dream of you into glorious light.

Your Father knows the beat of your heart when you have forgotten how to be. He knows the rhythm of your return when you don't know the road back. He knows the lyrics of why you are loved, when you can't remember quite how to live. He won't let you lose your way.

And when you have forgotten the words to His Word—to yourself—Jo will sing your Father's song for you, and you will be forever changed, undone, and remade. Jo takes your broken heart longing to break free, and she cups the dream of you close, and she whispers the words to you, so you can remember the refrain of you again and sing the song that was always meant to be yours before the beginning of time:

You know exactly how I was made, bit by bit,
how I was sculpted from nothing into something.
(Psalm 139)

I am completely God's masterpiece. (Ephesians 2:10)

I am completely forgiven. (Ephesians 1:7)

I am completely a new creature. (2 Corinthians 5:17)

I am completely strong in the Lord. (Ephesians 6:10)

I am completely accepted in Christ. (Ephesians 1:6)

I am completely loved with an everlasting love. (Jeremiah 31:3)

I am completely overtaken with blessings. (Deuteronomy 28:2)

And your Father and your sisters will sing it soft and strong and certain, of the dream of who you are, until you find your way again. Until you remember the notes of your song—one that awakens all of you to everything you ever dreamed of.

Find your realest identity—and you find how to be really free.

Lean into these soul-stirring pages that will just keep singing your song.

Tuning you to what grace is, awaking you to your soul's Lover who rejoices over you with gladness, who never stops singing the Belovedness of you, until every single one of your fears is quieted with His love, and the dream of you comes true.

—Ann Voskamp,
*New York Times* best-selling author of
*The Broken Way* and *One Thousand Gifts*

# Red Boots

In your wildest, most exciting dreams, who were you? Did any of those dreams ever come close to your reality?

When I was a little girl, about four years old, I wanted to be Wonder Woman. I didn't need to look like her, I wanted to *be* like her and live like she did. By day, she covered up her mysterious, powerful origins. To those around her, she was the understated and underestimated Diana Prince, a hardworking navy officer. Later she became an agent working for Inter-Agency Defense Command (a CIA/FBI–type agency). Yet in times of crisis, Diana's full identity was revealed. She would spin around and be transformed into Wonder Woman.

As Wonder Woman, Diana could leap a wall, communicate telepathically, and fly an invisible aircraft. Even her outfit (on occasion including a cape, a clear indicator of her superhero status) and her accessories possessed special crime-fighting powers. It never once occurred to me that perhaps she could have worn a few more clothes whilst fighting for justice. She was Wonder Woman; she could wear whatever she pleased!

My favorite part of her outfit was her red, knee-high boots. But what she wore didn't matter as much as the fact that Wonder Woman had passionate ideals and fought for justice and equality. She was beautiful, kind, thoughtful, and wise. Wonder Woman was changing the world, dealing with the bad guys, looking out for the good guys, and simply being amazing every single day.

I was in awe. Wonder Woman's adventurous life was my happily ever after. In my four-year-old mind, someday I would follow in her footsteps.

And then my Aunty May returned from a rummage sale with a pair of red leather Wonder Woman boots. They were for me! I don't think I could have loved May any more than I did on that day. The moment those boots touched my feet, I was no longer a little girl with big ideas and dreams and hopes. I was the Wonder Woman of my own world. I was mysterious, possessing secret insights and skills. I was strong, kind, and powerful, and I was going to change the world.

I wore my red boots as often as I was allowed, with any and every kind of outfit. Of course, the boots looked great with sweatpants. And yes, they matched my party dress perfectly. When I had my Wonder Woman boots on, I held my head high and walked taller. I was fearless. Wonder Woman expressed everything I wanted to be. And now with my boots on, Wonder Woman looked like me.

So it was quite possibly the saddest day of my childhood when, at age five, I realized how much my feet had grown. My Wonder Woman boots were two sizes too tight, and I finally had to let them go. My brief life as a superhero was over. My powers were gone, my mystery lost, my mission compromised.

I wasn't Wonder Woman anymore; I was just ordinary little me.

## What Was Your Dream of You?

Let's return to the question I asked at the beginning of this introduction: What was the dream you had of yourself from the very beginning? Before life interrupted, before anyone told you who you were allowed to be?

Take a moment now to recall the dreams you had, the dreams of who you could be.

There is something special and important about our unfiltered, innocent dreams. Even though they're also imperfect and naive in places, they can be signposts to our aspirations and hopes, our longings and ideals. They express something of who we are, they speak of our identity, maybe even hint at the kind of life we were made for.

You and I had an identity before anyone came along to tell us we couldn't be that person. We had a purpose long before experience told us we weren't worthy of one. We even had a voice, tiny though it might have been, before it was muted.

Yet as life unfolds, you hear voices telling you that you can't be the person you dreamed you'd become. Some are simply part of growing up. No, you are not Wonder Woman. No, your cape won't help you fly. No, you are not a princess, life is not a fairy tale, and you won't live in a beautiful castle. The more problematic voices are the ones that speak to your real identity and invalidate you. They sound authoritative: "You're a bit too assertive. Girls aren't supposed to be like that." They question your passion and vision, delegitimizing you with every sentence.

"Your dreams aren't in line with reality."

"Women are not meant to be strong."

"Those goals are way beyond your abilities."

"It's futile to try to fight injustice. There will *always* be injustice."

These voices limit us as they tell us what we can expect, and for some reason we believe them. So let me ask you: What happened to the dream of who you are—and why?

I can't stress enough how important it is to establish a secure and healthy understanding of your identity. You need to know who you are. This is not self-serving or the epitome of self-interest; it is essential to your well-being. Why? Because as Carol Dweck, Stanford psychology professor, has written, "[T]he view you adopt for yourself profoundly affects the way you lead your life. It can determine whether you become the person you want to be and whether you accomplish the things you value."[1]

The way you view yourself will define how you rest, work, and play; how you fight and make peace. It will shape the way you love. It influences how you approach your relationship with God. Your sense of identity flows into your relationships with others. For example, if you believe the lie that you're worthless, it will shape and distort your outlook on life. It will influence how you treat your body and how you allow other people to treat you.

Your understanding (or misunderstanding) of your identity will define your sense of purpose and your contribution to the world. It will tell you whether to value your talents or believe you have nothing of value to offer. What you believe about your identity will tell you whether you share your dreams and live as a woman directed by vision and mission, or whether to hide your dreams away believing they are pointless. It's impossible for you, me, or anyone else to live beyond what we believe to be true about ourselves.

When you are uncertain about who you are, you will believe—wrongly—that your value has to be earned. You will try to prove your worth through achievement. Your identity will be held in place by a fragile truce that comes with burdensome conditions, instead of a lasting peace and contentment that grounds your life. You will rely on the recognition and applause of others to center you and provide affirmation.

And what does all this do to you? You will exhaust yourself mentally, physically, and emotionally trying to earn the approval of people or institutions. Then you'll take yourself beyond exhaustion as you try to hold on to the approval you feel you have earned. You'll be trying so hard to keep it all together that you'll have no energy left to find your way back to who you truly are. You will have lost sight of the fullness of your true identity. You'll no longer see or believe the reality of your God-given potential and purpose.

It's time to stop the downward spiral and start living a different way.

It's time to recover the Dream of You.

## THE DREAM OF YOU

The Dream of You is not merely an expression of your wildest dreams and greatest aspirations; the Dream of You soars above your childhood dreams and icons—even though at times they can act as signposts to your deepest longings. The Dream of You is not just about who you think you are on a good day.

> The Dream of You is God's vision of you—your real, true identity and your God-given purpose.

It is not a dream that you have to earn, and it does not require that a vote be taken by others. It is bigger than the weighty burdens of obligations and expectations that you have encountered up to now.

The Dream of You is about being who you truly are and living the life you were made for. The Dream of You is God's vision of you—your real, true identity and your God-given purpose.

While life experiences, your environment, your cultural heritage, and your relationships all help shape you, the Dream of You takes into full account God's promise of redemption and transformation. It empowers you to let go of old, broken, and limited definitions of who you are so you are free to discover and learn how to live fully into who you really are.

Are you ready to recover and reclaim the Dream of You? Then let's start with where you are right now—with your identity and purpose today. As we do that, we'll consider how life brought you here.

# Don't Call Me "Pleasant"

HEY, FRIEND,

You are fully known and deeply loved by the living God.

You are seen, every single part of you.

You have a voice, you have ideas, you have a purpose.

You are valuable. You are worthy.

Just let all this sink in for a minute.

But somewhere along the way, you lost sight of the truth of who you are. You became who you thought you had to be. You became what was expected of you, what pleased the world around you, what people required of you. That was fine for a while; perhaps it was even necessary. That is, until you reached a place where you don't know who you are anymore. And you haven't been able to find your way back.

Most of the time, life is too full and moving too fast for you to even pay attention to the gradual loss of identity. But you can't escape the moments in life that reveal the situation. It's in the way you automatically second-guess your opinions. Or in the guilt you feel about your pride in your dreams and ideas of doing something big. It's revealed in the way you burn yourself out catering to the needs and wants of others. It's in the hope that by being and doing you will earn more love and acceptance. And when you have worn yourself out and still haven't received the recognition, you try even harder.

It's in the way you can't get beyond your past, and the stain of shame that you can't seem to escape. After all this time, you still wonder if God really could love someone like you.

I wrote this book for you.

It's the story of how identities get broken, but how they can be redeemed.

It's the story of how voices are muted, but how one day they sing a new song.

It's the story of how God transforms us so we can be free.

It's my story, and I believe it's yours too. It's a story that unfolds every day.

It is possible to find your way back to who you are and recover the life you were made for. It's not always easy, but the path is paved with God's grace and mercy. If you're ready for the journey, I'd love to walk alongside you and keep you company. We'll share our stories along the way. And maybe some snacks.

With love,

Jo

W ho do you think you are? It's a life-defining and an identity-defining question. When I consider who I think I am, what my identity is, I sometimes think I'm a woman simply trying to keep up with the expectations of the world around me.

Standing at an airport newsstand looking for some light reading, I noticed the glossy images on magazine covers. The cover models' features and dimensions defied gravity. There was not one photo of a person on any magazine cover that looked anything like me.

Then there were the claims made by magazine-cover headlines. I needed to buy one magazine to get a perfect body while another offered a must-read article that would teach me how to be the perfect parent and not ruin my children's lives. Forever.

Yet another magazine promised to make me amazing in bed, while the one just below it assured me I could make nutritious, locally sourced meals in only fifteen minutes. An entire section of magazines pointed out all the accessories I needed to own for the perfectly appointed home. How would I afford all this? Thankfully, another magazine contained the skills I needed to become a multimillionaire entrepreneur.

To ward off any doubts that all this was possible and could be accomplished *now,* the magazines featured beautiful people who had achieved these goals by the time they were twenty-five. I should simply have walked away from this madness, but I couldn't help myself.

I said rather loudly, "All I want is a bloody magazine!" and walked away with nothing but angst.

It's not just me, and it's not just you. It has to do with being a woman in a society that refuses to accept and celebrate women on their own merits. Our society seems far more interested in limiting us to role definitions that usually have little to do with the qualities, intelligence, and talent we each uniquely bring to the world.

Marketing analyst Clotaire Rapaille has written, "Being a woman in America is difficult. . . . So many rules, so many tensions."[1] I agree, except I'd add that my sisters around the world know this is not an issue only in America. Globally, in different cultures and different ways, we're all feeling the pressure to conform to imposed standards designed to limit us. We all wrestle with a range of rules and expectations and have to work against the voices that keep telling us who we're supposed to be and what we're supposed to live for.

As we have seen, our sense of identity is shaped by far more than childhood dreams. Some of us were given inaccurate identities when life interrupted and distracted us. The people around us have left their mark. And personal experiences don't remain in the past. They leave a deep imprint, forever changing us.

## WHEN LIFE CHANGES YOUR NAME

In ancient times, a woman named Naomi left her homeland along with her husband and sons. They moved to Moab to escape famine, and they hoped it would be an opportunity to make a new beginning. Sadly, life didn't turn out the way Naomi had hoped. In Moab, she lost her husband and both her sons. She returned home years later with a daughter-in-law, Ruth. When they reached Naomi's hometown, the community welcomed her back. But devastated by grief, Naomi was no longer the woman they had known years before.

"Don't call me Naomi," she told the people. [Naomi means "pleasant."] "Instead, call me Mara [meaning "bitter"], for the Almighty has made life very bitter for me. I went away full, but the LORD has brought me home empty" (Ruth 1:20–21).

Naomi's sorrow changed her life and renamed her identity. Yet it's not only the life-shattering events that shape our identities.

Another story from ancient times shows that allowing others to define one's identity can sideline even a person marked for royalty. Saul, about to be appointed king of Israel, failed to show up for his own coronation. His unexpected disappearance was so concerning that the people sought God to find the king. The response: "He is hiding among the baggage" (1 Samuel 10:22). Saul eventually came out from his hiding place to assume leadership of the nation, but he never escaped the baggage of his own insecurities.

If you read his story in the Bible, you'll see that insecurity and other issues buried Saul's potential. He lived for the approval of others, even at the expense of obeying God. For instance, the king felt so threatened by a young newcomer named David that he tried to kill him. The attempts on David's life continued for years. Saul's insecurity was a toxin that overwhelmed his identity and poisoned his life.

It's human to experience insecurity. We don't feel confident all the time, and it's tempting to compare ourselves with other people. Yet the insecurities, if left unaddressed, can grow from momentary emotions to a definitive worldview that determines how we feel, think, and act. Insecurity becomes our identity.

If personal experiences, the interruptions of life, and the voices of those around us have poisoned who we really are, how can you find out your true identity? You know the "right" answer as well as I do. Knowing Jesus forms the basis of your identity, and having a personal knowledge of Him changes everything. Doesn't it?

Doesn't it?

## WHY THE BIG DISCONNECT?

For many of us, knowing Jesus has not pointed the way to finding out who we truly are. How can that be possible? Perhaps it's because humans find it hard to receive love, gifts, and kindness. We have trouble accepting grace. Maybe after all of our achievements in culture, arts, technology, and science, we assume we now have to overachieve in the realms of spirituality and faith. As a result, our identity in Christ becomes yet another task to add to an overcrowded list of jobs to get done.

Wash the car.

Fold the laundry.

Pick up prescriptions.

Be like Jesus.

Before we know it, a life-changing, heart-transforming, identity-defining relationship with the living God through Jesus Christ is reduced to a formulaic "to achieve" list. The list often includes attending church regularly, participating in mid-week groups, giving money and time, maintaining personal piety and devotion, and helping others—especially those who are less well off. Of course, it involves being a generally "nice" and vaguely "moral" person. These activities are good, even great things. It's just that these are things to do. They are not who you *are*.

When our identity in Christ is reduced to a checklist, it's no wonder the connection between our faith and our identity is, instead, a big disconnect for many of us. Surely seeking to be defined as a follower of Jesus is not just more empty hype.

We know that Jesus is the answer, so we feel vague guilt about challenging the assertion that he is *the* answer. But if Jesus answers the question, "Who are you?" then why are we still struggling to find our deepest, truest identities? Where are the freedom, peace, and security that were promised? We've sung it, we've read it, we've stood on the promise of it, and even though we know on some level these things must be true, they don't seem to be true for us.

We still don't know who we are. Some of us, not having found a way to get past the experiences that defined us, identify with Naomi. Some of us align with Saul: We haven't been able to break out from the baggage of our insecurities. We have been trapped in comparing and competing, neither of which can end well. We have listened to other definitions of who we are, and paying attention to the voices has limited our potential and our future. Maybe, as the voices tell us, the problem is *us*. Once again, we're not good enough.

Thankfully, God sees us from a completely different vantage point.

## God's Design for Glorious Living

> It's in Christ that we find out who we are and what we
> are living for. Long before we first heard of Christ and
> got our hopes up, he had his eye on us, had designs on
> us for glorious living, part of the overall purpose he is
> working out in everything and everyone. (Ephesians
> 1:11–12, MSG)

The Scripture passage is not a slogan; it's the truth. This is the answer to the heartache behind our deepest longings, the answer to the stories behind our wildest dreams. This truth is the answer to our hopes for who we really are and can become. There is so much more to discover than rules and tensions. Before we even knew Jesus, He had designs on us for glorious living.

The words of truth regarding your identity were written by a man named Paul, a zealous persecutor of Christians until he met Jesus in a life-transforming, literally blinding, encounter. The passage forms part of a letter written to church communities in the ancient city of Ephesus (in modern-day Turkey) and the surrounding region. Paul's letter communicated deep truths that still apply to all believers.

The cosmopolitan city of Ephesus experienced something of an awakening to the good news of the gospel when Paul and his team preached there (see Acts 19). People from all backgrounds and walks of life came to faith. Incredible miracles took place. People who had been involved in witchcraft burned their books and tools and became Christians. Others publicly confessed their wrongdoing. This kind of public confession bore particular significance in this city. Ephesus was home to many religious temples, but its preeminent shrine was the Temple of Diana, still considered to be one of the seven wonders of the ancient world. The Temple of Diana also was known to be a place of sanctuary and asylum. People could find immunity there, escaping the consequences of their crimes.[2]

The Temple of Diana played a huge role in the city's cultural life, housing its arts scene. The worship of Diana, which fueled the local economy, included rituals and practices that exploited women as temple prostitutes. As pagan worshippers of Diana responded to the gospel and started following Jesus, a decline in commerce derived from former temple-goers affected local businesses. Business owners who were losing profits eventually incited a riot against Paul.

Paul and his team decided to leave, eventually moving on to Macedonia (see Acts 20) and Greece. Meanwhile, new converts living in a pagan land were figuring out what their faith meant to their everyday lives. They were dealing with opposition and conflict due to their faith in Jesus Christ. These men and women were Christians who had left behind a life that bore little similarity to a life in Christ. They needed guidance.

That's why Paul pointed out in the first chapter of his letter to the Ephesians that a new life with Jesus is exactly that: a completely new life. This is huge in orienting believers in the way to live in a hostile culture (see Acts 19). It also was freeing for the Ephesians. It meant that people who had lived in spiritual darkness, putting their trust in a religion that was powerless to help them, no longer had to be defined by the past. God was making them new, from the inside out.

Can you imagine what it is like to let go of everything that is familiar in order to fully embrace a new life? This means laying down the old way of living, including friends, family, community, the way you used to think, your worldview—all the things that had made you *you*. The old life can't continue to exist alongside the new life. But forsaking the old life means having all your comforts and reference points stripped away. With all that left behind, who are you now and what are you living for?

Try to put yourself in the place of converts to the Christian faith who had spent their lives practicing a pagan religion. They sought a change, and now they were experiencing a complete turnaround. Think of the challenges they faced in changing their lives—and staying changed.

We've all tried to reboot our lives at some point: a juice cleanse to reboot our health, a decluttering session to clear out our homes. Or maybe a commitment to stick to a New Year's resolution with the promise of a "New Year, New You." A word to live by each year to help you remember the person you've always wanted to be and the life you've hoped to live.

I'm a huge fan of New Year's resolutions, the chance to start again, the chance to transform my life. My attempts have met with varying degrees of success. The weight I lost one year found its way home again. Career paths sometimes took me in a direction I hadn't planned to take. The determination to be a better woman (whatever that meant) brought me—exhausted—face to face with who I am. My resolve to change my life never has been enough. I've needed something lasting and someone bigger than me.

## In Christ = In Covenant Relationship

Throughout the Bible we read of people who discovered that a relationship with God transformed all of life—including their identities—from the inside out. This transformative relationship is possible because of God's covenant promise, a consistent theme that conveys the freedom in our new identity. Covenants were common in the culture of Old Testament times.

Agreements between two people or between tribes, when one party was stronger than the other, often were marked by a ceremony in which an animal was sacrificed. The stronger party took the initiative to cancel the other party's debt, freeing the weaker party from the burdens and consequences they faced. The stronger party gave the new covenant partner a new identity. Their past was over. They were given a new name that reflected who and whose they now were.

As a result of the covenant, the weaker party assumes the attributes of the stronger partner. The weaker party never would be alone and vulnerable again, because the covenant bestowed a new life and a new place of belonging. As a tangible reminder of all that the covenant meant, the agreement was marked by a scar, often formed by a cut on the wrist. The scar also served to warn potential adversaries that the person carrying the scar was in covenant relationship. If weaker covenant partners were attacked, they had a stronger partner who would come to their defense.[3]

In the Bible we see God enter into covenant relationship with His people, including Abram and Sarai, Noah, Moses, and David. All of these covenants pointed to a greater One. The ancient covenants eventually were fulfilled in the life, death, and resurrection of Jesus.

As the stronger covenant partner, God took the initiative by entering into a relationship with a broken humanity. He sent His Son, Jesus, whose life illustrates what a relationship with God and what an identity in God is like. The covenant that transforms our lives is not enacted in the sacrifice of an animal, as was done in Old Testament times. Instead, Jesus Himself (described by John the Baptist as "The Lamb of God who takes away the sin of the world!" [John 1:29]) is the sacrifice, laying down His life for us. His body—not the bodies of the weaker covenant partners—carries the scars in His side and in His hands. His death breaks the power of the debt we owed by canceling the penalty for our sin. Now humanity, the weaker covenant partner, has new life and a new place of belonging.

We are no longer defined or named by our past. Instead, we have been given a new identity. We're in Christ now. We have access to the attributes of our stronger covenant Partner. This covenant means God's redemption is at work in every part of life. In biblical terms, *redemption* means "the buying back of something that has been lost." People who have been lost through helplessness, poverty, violence, and foolishness are bought back. It also means "deliverance from bondage, freed from everything that enslaves and controls us." Redemption was good news for God's covenant people in the Old Testament. Redemption was good news for the people of Ephesus who never had heard of Christ until they met Paul. Redemption is good news for us and our identity and purpose because it changes everything.

Jesus not only rescued us from the debt we never could repay. He also paid the price for all that we had lost due to the reality of a broken world. In His death and resurrection, He broke every chain that held us captive. You may know already that He has rescued you. You may know that He has forgiven you. But you also need to know that His redemption of your life has transformative implications for your identity. You no longer have to accept lies about who you are. You have a new identity. In Christ you find out who you are and what you are living for.

He doesn't shame or condemn you for your past. He breaks the chains of all that controlled you and limited your identity. He redeems your true identity, which was interrupted by your life experiences and crushed by the mixed messages of the world. He even redeems the dreams you had of the person you hoped to become. He redeems your Dream of You.

That said, He has way more in mind for you than a pair of red boots; He has designs on you for glorious living. Redemption means He makes all things new.

## REDEEMED TO RECLAIM YOUR TRUE IDENTITY

Christ invites us to discover who we are. And because we have a relationship with God, this discovery is an ongoing process. We can learn to let go of the broken identities that have wrongly defined us. But we also can revisit areas of our identities that bear further exploration. God has led me to revisit the same areas of my identity in different seasons of my life. How my body image affected my identity as a lithe metabolic wonder at age nineteen is not the same for me now. Today my body image has to do with being a woman in her forties, after having two children, with decades of love for fried chicken, and with a metabolism that decided to go on a *long,* slow vacation. It's a different deal.

God has needed to redeem my long-held identification with Wonder Woman in every decade of my life. The Wonder Woman of my childhood was a little adventurer. In my teens she was the girl who became obsessed with academic excellence and was determined to have the chance to create her own dreams in the face of discrimination. The Wonder Woman of my twenties sought to be accomplished, hot (attractive, not sweaty), and married. The Wonder Woman of my thirties aimed to be the perfect wife and mother with a perfect home and career.

And today? I'm doing great, thanks very much. I could use a long nap, and I wouldn't mind a new pair of fantastic red leather boots. That's all the Wonder I've got energy for.

> Long before we first heard of Christ, He had His eye on us. He had designs on us for glorious living.

One final thing to remember: while the work of redemption is incredibly liberating, it's also incredibly costly. Our redemption was wrought on a cross, a humiliating, agonizing form of execution. As we journey with Jesus, sometimes we'll feel relief and freedom, a weight lifted off our shoulders, gladly resting in the hands of our stronger covenant Partner. At other times, as redemption works on the deepest parts of who we are, we'll journey to painful places, the kinds of places that disciples are tempted to run away from. We'll be tempted to avoid the vulnerability and nakedness. We'll be tempted to hide to keep anyone from seeing us bleed. We'll be tempted to avoid bringing the broken pieces of our identities to the Cross. There will be times where we'll be tempted to rationalize, minimize, or ignore our culpability, or our own sin. We'll be tempted to comfort and appease ourselves, rather than deny ourselves and choose to stop going our own way (see Matthew 16:24). At those times, going back to living by the *oughts* and *shoulds* of our culture and giving in to our insecurities will feel a lot easier, even more appealing!

It will be important to remember that the Cross is not the end, but rather what happens before resurrection, before new life. Remind yourself that when the grit and the guts of your broken identity meet the grace and goodness of God, it will reveal you, but He will transform you. You're in Him now, with all His resources available to you. You have access to His power, mercy, and grace.

Sometimes you'll feel impatient with the process, wondering why it demands so much. You'll be frustrated that transformation and growth are such slow, hard work. Surely, you will conclude, if Jesus has secured your freedom, it shouldn't feel so difficult and take so long.

Yet this new covenant is more than a spiritual transaction, a contract that was signed when we first heard about Jesus. It's a relationship with the living God that grows, stretches, and deepens over time. When Paul wrote to another church community, describing the difference this new covenant makes, he stated that it "makes us more and more like him as we are changed into his glorious image" (2 Corinthians 3:18). We have the opportunity to continually respond to the covenant love that God offers us through Jesus.

Discover the depth of your identity in Christ as you let go of the old life of trying to prove yourself worthy, of striving to measure up to an imposed standard. Embrace your covenant relationship in all its fullness. Invite God into your past life experiences and ask Him to break you free from the debts, the brokenness, and the wasted years. It's in Christ that we find out who we are and what we are living for. Long before we first heard of Christ, He had His eye on us. He had designs on us for glorious living. Discover His Dream of You and His dreams for you.

As we wrap up this chapter, take a few moments to pause and reflect on what a covenant relationship with God could mean for your identity and purpose.

# What's in a Name?

HEY, SISTER,

When I was pregnant, I would pore over pages of books searching for the perfect names for my soon-to-arrive children. As a child I had attended celebratory naming ceremonies for the newborns in our Nigerian community. So when it came to naming my own children, I had specific goals. A name needed to be timeless and perhaps capture a yet-unseen personality as indicated by a baby's in utero behaviors. (One of my children would kick at the same times, three times a day. The other somersaulted on no established schedule.)

Above all, a name should help tell a person's story. My husband and I formed a multiethnic family, so our children's names needed to reflect our wide, rich story.

Still, those who know me well would tell you that my name-centered goals go well beyond naming children. They'll tell you that I'm a little obsessed with naming. Every friend I have is given a new nickname. I happily name everything I have: events, parties, cars, guitars . . . iPods. I admit this *might* be a problem.

Everything needs a title, a definition. On long walks and in late-night conversations, I have told close friends about the names I was called, things that were said to me and about me. Sticks and stones didn't break my bones, but names could always hurt me. These names would leave their mark. They would wrongly define me.

Being wrongly named can cause you to walk a little bent over. It's as though the words, the labels, the definitions press on you so heavily they drag you down. The false labels have caused you not to live by your given name, which merely introduces you. Words and experiences limit who you try to be and who you are trying not to be, to the extent that you don't know who you really are.

It doesn't have to stay this way. Walk through these next few pages with me, read these words into the night if you need to. They will remind you of One who is truth, overcoming all the powerful lies you've lived under. He knows your true name, and He will lift your head and straighten your back.

xo,

Jo

❧

It's dusk, yet another hot and dusty evening. From where he stands in his room near the palace, he looks out over the city. He sees torches flicker in the distance, and he inhales the smell of this land that is far from his original home.

He wears the clothes of the powerful, the trappings of an official whose authority is second only to that of Pharaoh. He smiles, bemused to think that the lavish coat his father gave him when he was young was nothing compared to this. Yet the coat that had been given to him in love had sent him into so much trouble.

Voices come to him, the sounds of his children squealing as they play. His smile broadens and thoughts of his sons crowd out any further thoughts about his past. Joseph turns and goes inside to find his boys. There is no need to dwell on the troubles and pain of his youth.

## JOSEPH, A MAN WITH A SHIFTING IDENTITY

Thanks to Sunday school storybooks and Andrew Lloyd Webber's musical about an amazing Technicolor dreamcoat, Joseph, son of Jacob, is one of the most familiar biblical figures in popular culture. His story is told through thirteen chapters in the book of Genesis. Joseph was his father's favorite, much to the annoyance of his brothers. His father so indulged his eleventh son that he gave Joseph an ornate coat—the kind reserved for supervisors. Meanwhile, Joseph's older brothers were sent to tend the flocks.[1]

Not only was Joseph favored; he was gifted. He had supernatural dreams that revealed his future leadership role, but as a young man he lacked the emotional intelligence to realize that boasting about his dreams offended his family. His jealous and vindictive brothers tossed him into a pit and sold him to slavers. To cover up their violence, the brothers put blood on Joseph's coat and led their father to conclude that Joseph had been killed by wild animals (see Genesis 37:31–33).

The slave traders later sold Joseph, and he ended up in Egypt, which at that time was the world's superpower. Joseph served in the household of Potiphar, the captain of Pharaoh's guard. It's hard to imagine more jarring circumstances for Joseph to be in, but the narrative tells us, "The LORD was with Joseph, so he succeeded in everything he did as he served in the home of his Egyptian master" (Genesis 39:2).

Potiphar realized that he was being blessed by God's presence in Joseph's life. As Joseph continued to succeed, the captain's home and business flourished. So Potiphar gave Joseph successive promotions until finally, the captain of the guard gave Joseph administrative oversight over everything he owned (see Genesis 39:3–6). After the horrors of being sold into slavery, Joseph's life was finally getting somewhere.

Then Potiphar's wife tried to seduce the young man. When he refused her advances and ran away, she falsely accused him of rape. Joseph lost everything to yet another injustice. This time he was thrown in jail.

While in prison he interpreted dreams for members of the palace staff. This gift eventually put him in the presence of Pharaoh, who had been troubled by his own dreams. Joseph's gift of interpreting dreams led to a position of prominence in Egypt—a post second in power only to Pharaoh himself. Ultimately, the God-given dreams of leadership and influence that Joseph had as a young man were fulfilled.

The story gets even better when a famine drives Jacob's sons to visit Joseph without realizing who the "Egyptian" official really is. The brothers who had sold Joseph and then lied to their father now depended on him to keep their family from starvation.

## WHY NAMES MATTER

We are given few glimpses into Joseph's interior life during his journey. But when he named his children, it revealed the depth of his growth.

> Before the years of famine came, two sons were born to
> Joseph by Asenath daughter of Potiphera, priest of On.
> Joseph named his firstborn Manasseh and said, "It is
> because God has made me forget all my trouble and all my
> father's household." The second son he named Ephraim
> and said, "It is because God has made me fruitful in the
> land of my suffering." (Genesis 41:50–52, NIV)

In biblical times, a name carried profound significance. It spoke of a person's family and heritage, but also the person's character, potential, and purpose.

> A good name is more desirable than great riches;
>     to be esteemed is better than silver or gold. (Proverbs
> 22:1, NIV)

Sometimes a name reflected the parents' circumstances. Joseph's name emerged through his mother, Rachel, and stepmother (and aunt), Leah. The two women competed for the affections of their husband, Jacob. Leah was Jacob's first wife, but he gave preferential treatment to her younger sister Rachel. Leah named her firstborn Reuben, which sounds like the Hebrew for "the LORD has seen my misery" (NIV). Leah said of Reuben's name, "The LORD has noticed my misery, and now my husband will love me" (Genesis 29:32).

One of Rachel's sons conceived through a surrogate was named Naphtali, meaning "my struggle." She said, "I have struggled hard with my sister, and I'm winning!" (Genesis 30:8). When Rachel finally gave birth to a son, she named him Joseph, meaning "may he add." Of Joseph, Rachel said, "May the LORD add yet another son to my family" (Genesis 30:24).

A name also could speak of a person's character. Jacob, Joseph's father, came out of the womb grasping his older twin's heel. So he was named Jacob, meaning "he grasps the heel." The phrase was a Hebrew idiom for "he deceives" or "he takes advantage of." Both idioms were true of Jacob's character.

A child's name was a declaration of his or her identity. For many leading characters of the Old Testament, their names defined their lives. When Joseph named his sons, he declared in advance a God-given identity over them that spoke of Joseph's redemption. Joseph named his older son Manasseh, a word that sounds like a Hebrew term meaning "causing to forget" (see Genesis 41:51). He named his second son Ephraim, a name that sounds like a Hebrew term that means "fruitful" (see Genesis 41:52). The names of these sons later became the names of two of the twelve tribes of Israel.

The God who had kept covenant with Joseph as he endured abuse, enslavement, and betrayal helped Joseph forget (Manasseh) his struggles and sorrows. The foreign land that had become his home was no longer a place of despair, loss, and horror. It had become fruitful *(Ephraim)*. Not just for Joseph, but also for his extended family and his adopted nation.

What is most remarkable about the naming of Joseph's sons is where it's placed in the bigger story. Joseph's wise leadership rescued Egypt during seven years of famine. His administration of the country's resources had strengthened Egypt's economic position in the region as travelers from famine-ravaged nations visited Egypt to purchase food and supplies. Furthermore, Joseph eventually was reunited with his father and reconciled with his brothers.

Yet Joseph named his sons before any of those events took place. His sons' names declare that Joseph already was free, whole, and living the God-given life he was made for. He did not allow the past to name him, as had happened with Naomi, who returned home telling her former neighbors to call her Mara (bitterness). Events that stole so much from Joseph did not have the last word in his life. The fruits of restoration overflowed from his life, blessing everyone around him.

His mother, Rachel, had given Joseph a name meaning "may he add" (see Genesis 30:24). God answered her prayer yet again by giving her one more son, Benjamin (see Genesis 35:18). But God also added to Joseph's life by way of sons, prestige, influence, and power, as well as through redemption and restoration.

## WHAT NAME DO YOU LIVE BY?

When we're getting to know a person, we often ask about the person's name. Are you named for a relative? What would your name have been if you had been born a different gender? We are naturally curious about the circumstances surrounding the person's name.

However, as you explore and reclaim your own identity, perhaps the more telling questions to ask are "Who named you?" and "What named you?" What experience, situation, or relationship has defined your understanding of your identity and potential?

The names given to me at birth tell you only so much of who I am. Through a set of circumstances beyond my control, I later found that my soul, my heart, and my thoughts—my whole life—had been named in a more definitive way.

My earliest memories are recalled visually in a summer haze. I'm sitting in a garden surrounded by huge, pretty rosebushes. I'm making things—a fort, a mud pie, a magic wand—as I enact my adventurous dreams. Or I'm talking to my chickens in the backyard, asking about their day. Or I'm climbing on my very patient dog, trying to will her into assuming her true destiny as a magnificent Pegasus for my Wonder Woman.

As you explore and reclaim your own identity, perhaps the more telling questions to ask are "Who named you?" and "What named you?"

In my earliest memories, the sun is shining and I feel warm and safe. Secure. It plays like an old home-recorded film clip. I can see the colors of the setting and the movements of the people.

Reality tends to paint a starker picture than the one given to us by our memories. For instance, my memories often fail to articulate that my warm, summer-haze memory-picture takes place in foster care. This detail gets left out largely because it was a normal living arrangement for me. It was the only life I could recall, since years earlier my parents' marriage and our family had fragmented across two continents.

A nice yet random lady used to come to our foster home to visit me and ask questions. She was my social worker. The fuller picture showed a diverse foster family. There was my brother. Then my foster mother, Aunty May, an elderly, unmarried, white woman. My foster brothers also were white. The picture included lively and enjoyable visits from my mom and my Aunty Bassey. Aunty May always made a special trifle on those days. Still, the overriding visual that stands out is that my foster home was home, that Aunty May was home, and it was summer. Warm. Safe. Secure.

That is, until December 11, 1979, when the warm, summery, hazy days of memory were replaced. (In truth, I don't know if that was the exact December day, but in my mind that is the date stamp.)

It was snowing. Normally that didn't matter since I loved playing in the snow. I loved it when the snow was so deep it reached my thighs. I loved snowflakes and snowmen and snowballs and snow angels. I'd open my arms and lift my face to the sky, daring the snow to come and get me. I loved the chill feel of flakes falling on my eyelids, providing frosty white eyelashes on my dark brown skin. I loved the gentle teasing of melting flakes on my tongue. I'd jump and squeal and fall into its fun.

But the day that appears in my memory was different. The scene is set in slow motion.

It was snowing hard, flakes so full and thick they overpowered everything, silencing the street with their weight. It was bitterly cold. The wind stung my face and held me back. Winter didn't want to play with me that day.

I don't remember a goodbye. I don't remember looking back and waving through the rear window. I don't remember if my brother spoke, or if anyone did. I just remember that it was bitterly cold and there was a lot of snow. Soon I was in a taxi, then on a train. There were no tears. Why would there be? It was a familiar trip. I was headed back to London where I was born, but not home, I mean the home identified with Aunty May. I was headed somewhere different for the Christmas holidays.

There I was standing amid towering grown-ups with familial, yet unfamiliar, faces as the adults welcomed me home. At first I was confused. Why did they think I was home? Then I realized they were serious about celebrating my homecoming.

Home?

The raw elements of winter had tried to warn me. The cold stood still and mourned. The snow slowed me down and then sorrowfully buried me, snowflake by snowflake. My story and my life as I knew them were being buried. I hadn't been told that I was leaving Aunty May's house for good, that I would never again live with her. Somehow the big goodbye had happened without me, even though I was right there.

I didn't cry. I was both happy and sad. I was happy to be with my family. I was home, and yet I wanted to go home. All I could think of were the gifts left underneath our Christmas tree at Aunty May's house. I knew, I just knew that one of them was the doll I had been promised, the doll I'd always wanted. Next to my doll were toys I'd play with, games I'd play with my friends. They were my presents. My name was written on them. They never came to my new home in London.

I was five years old, but the experience of leaving Aunty May's and arriving to what my family called "home" reshaped my identity. The grief and confusion I felt were way too big for my five-year-old heart to understand. This sudden shift was too complex for my five-year-old mind to interpret. All that was left was to react to it, and it defined me in a way that renamed me. It changed who I was. Starting at that moment, I saw the world differently.

I didn't like winter anymore. It was cold and dangerous. The wind stung me; snowflakes were annoying, frightening little things that became a big thing that could steal your world away. I resolved that when I grew up I would live in a place where the sun shone and it was always summer. I think I wanted summer because summer felt safe. I even became suspicious of Christmas holidays. What was the point of the gifts and the excitement? Why feel, again and again, the sadness of gifts that never came?

The changed, renamed me understood that life was . . . temporary. Homes were temporary. Relationships, even the very closest ones, were temporary. Life could change at any time without warning, leaving me sad, confused, and hurting. Better to be prepared. I trained my heart to keep people at a distance, because no matter how secure I felt, I didn't belong to anyone, not really. In the end, the people I loved could let me go. So I believed they always would.

## WHEN A NAME DEFINES YOUR LIFE

Who named you? Was it your family, your friends, your boss, your spouse? Maybe, like my experience, the renaming happened when you were very young. Children have little control over such powerful experiences, and yet the impact can resonate for the rest of one's life. Abuse, loss, loneliness. Some renaming events may seem minor but carry a heavy weight with them.

Years ago, I asked women at a Bible study how they were named and how the naming impacted their lives. Their answers were revealing.

"I'm the youngest in my family," said Joan, "so growing up I was immature and silly, somewhat frivolous. However, the label stuck, and no matter what I did, the attitude [toward me] remained." Her face flushed and her voice cracked with frustration. "Years later my siblings, and in fact no one in my family, takes what I say seriously. I'm still seen as silly. And I'm a grandmother."

Perhaps we've been named by an opinion about us that was expressed by someone who didn't really know us. The assessment of who we are—good or bad—shaped us and limited us.

Marie said, "When I was younger I was known in my group of friends as 'the skinny one.'" She paused, smirked, and looked around the room. "Then I had children. No one calls me the skinny one anymore!" The room erupted into laughter.

"I'm the strong one," said Clare. I noted that several women in the group murmured in agreement. It seems "the strong one" is a common name assigned to women. "I don't always feel strong, but I feel that that is what is expected of me. I know it's meant as a compliment, because I am capable and I support people. Sometimes I just wish someone would be the strong one for me."

I heard the group exhale, almost sighing in agreement.

Which "one" were you? The rebellious one, the happy one, the reliable one, the strong one, the sensible one, the cynical one? How has your name shaped your identity? How has it limited you?

## LETTING GO OF OLD NAMES

I had been defined by my early experience. For me, people and places were temporary. I would fall back on my personal history whenever I checked out of close friendships. "Sorry, I'm just really independent, always have been, going back to my foster days. It's nothing personal, it's just who I am."

On one level that was true. There was no point in pretending that the things that had named me didn't exist. I needed to face that reality. Yet I couldn't ignore that throughout biblical history, God transformed people. In many instances, even the circumstances that named them gave them a fresh identity and purpose. Abram and Sarai were transformed into Abraham and Sarah (see Genesis 17:5, 15), their new names reflecting their relationship with the living God and the promise of a son and a future lineage. Simon was renamed Peter after acknowledging Jesus as the Messiah (see John 1:42). His new name meant "little rock," speaking of his relationship with God (the Rock) but also of his future role in the church. God changed the names of people and in doing so changed their stories.

He could do the same for me.

The story of Jacob, Joseph's father, illustrates the raw reality of shedding an old name and receiving a new one. Jacob was forced to face his difficult and deceptive past when he encountered God on the bank of a river, and the encounter renamed Jacob forever. He was henceforth known as Israel, a name that later identified a nation (see Genesis 32:28).

On the bank of a river, a stranger confronted Jacob and fought with him. Muscle for muscle, strength for strength, it seemed the men were evenly matched. Neither man relented, so they fought through the night, bloodied and bruised. Suddenly this strange man, seeing that Jacob refused to let go, touched Jacob's hip and dislocated it.

They were not so evenly matched after all. Understand that this fight could have been over with a single touch at the very beginning. The man had decided to leave, but Jacob kept him there. "I will not let you go unless you bless me," Jacob told the strange man (Genesis 32:26). Jacob knew this mystery stranger was more than a man. He had encountered the Divine.

Jacob did receive his requested blessing, but he would walk with a limp for the rest of his life. Yet hadn't there always been something broken about Jacob? The events that brought him to this moment told his story and reflected his original name: Jacob, meaning "he who deceives, he who takes advantage" (see Genesis 25:26). He had deceived and taken advantage of his brother Esau, stealing the older brother's birthright and taking Esau's rightful blessing from their father, Isaac. Then he had to run for his life.

Jacob had been deceived and taken advantage of by his Uncle

Laban, given in marriage to one of Laban's daughters, a woman he didn't love. Then Jacob was forced to serve double the time to secure his marriage to Rachel, the woman he'd asked to marry all along. This was his life and there was nowhere left to run.

On the bank of a river, the stranger spoke to Jacob.

"What is your name?" (Genesis 32:27).

Who are you apart from the wealth you have earned, your flocks, and your possessions?

What is your name?

Jacob was set to meet up with his estranged brother the following day. But in this moment at the river, God brought a different kind of reckoning.

"Jacob," he said to the stranger (Genesis 32:27). "I'm Jacob."

I am Jacob. I'm a liar. I'm a cheat. I'm "he who deceives." Face to face with the powerful stranger, Jacob finally owned his name.

Then the man said, "Your name will no longer be Jacob, but Israel, because you have struggled with God and with men and have overcome" (Genesis 32:28, NIV).

Jacob was renamed Israel, meaning "God fights, struggles, prevails" or in other translations, "God's prince." The old name is gone. Jacob needed to be blessed with a new name. Yes, he was broken and he needed the blessing of a new identity.

He would walk differently from now on.

## DISCOVER GOD'S NEW NAME FOR YOU

God is still changing names and changing stories.

It took time for me to walk away from the experiences that

named me. It's almost instinctive to walk in the groove of habits that began in childhood. It has been a long, hard session of wrestling with God to come to the end of myself and yet not let go until God blesses me. Moving forward has meant walking with a limp, aware of my weakness and vulnerability. Still, the limp has created a dependence on God's Word and His Spirit's power to transform me. He is redeeming my story.

Having looked at the power of names and the importance of naming and being named, stop and give careful thought to the impact your name has on you now and has had on you in the past.

- Whoever or whatever has named you does not have to define you forever. Are you ready to discover your identity and purpose, your name? As a first step, carve out time to be alone with God.
- Tell God who and what has named you, and who you have become as a result. Feel free to wrestle in prayer for as long as it takes.
- Invite God to reveal the identity He has given you. This is the name that will give you new life.
- Don't be afraid if you feel vulnerable when you begin to embrace your new name. It's an opportunity to lean on God and to rely on His Word and power. He is redeeming your story.

# The Talk

SISTER, I SEE YOU.

You're driven. You're ambitious, always an over-achiever though you don't personally feel that you are. Whether you're a stay-at-home mom or a living-at-the-top-of-the-corporate-ladder careerist or a woman juggling the commitments of family and work, you're the kind of woman often described in superlatives. No one knows how you do it all. In truth you don't know either; this is just your normal. You do it because you do.

And because it is your normal, you don't give much thought to what it's like to live in your shoes. Always walking farther, harder, faster. Most of the time when you're moving this fast, you feel invigorated and alive, on course to reach your goals.

Until you're *always* running and you feel that if you were to slow down it all would collapse.

How does it feel to live in your shoes? Chances are you don't fully know. Your role hasn't been to think of your own needs. You wanted to honor the hard work and sacrifices of those who went before you. You wanted to realize the potential they said was in you.

Then there were those who refused to see you because they were locked into their perceptions of you. Or simply so preoccupied with seeing all that you do for them, they had no interest in valuing who you actually are. So your days have been defined by what you needed to do to silence their voices inside you and shatter the ceilings that held you back.

I see you. I see the way you are bone tired. I see that you feel lonely at times. I see that you love your life and yet wish it were different. I see you take a deep breath and carry on with the day's responsibilities. It's hard to think about reclaiming your unique identity.

Sister, you need to know this: The "ordinary" you, the person you were before all the achievement and recognition, was already extraordinary. Before you had to be and do what others required to even notice you, you were already worthy. You were already enough.

Would you be willing to go with me to look at the situation again? Would you be willing to take the risk to reclaim your true identity, to learn how it feels to be free? Let's get started.

Jo

❧

Long Live Queen Esther!"
Esther stood before the cheering crowds celebrating the holiday held in her honor.

First of all, my child, think magnificently of God,
Magnify His Providence; adore His power;
pray to Him frequently and incessantly.
Bear Him always in your mind. Teach
your thoughts to reverence Him in every
Place for there is no place where He is not.
Therefore, my child, fear & worship & love God;
first and last, think magnificently of Him.

Paternus
Advice to a Son

1600

She stood regal and revered, poised and beautiful. She smiled and gestured as she'd been taught.

The king and his dignitaries grinned at each other. She was everything they wanted her to be, everything they had worked toward. It was perfect; the Persian Empire had its new queen.

However, there was a problem, even though it wasn't the kind that the king, his officials, or the crowds cared to think about.

Esther was the most powerful and popular woman in the Persian Empire, everything the people dreamed of. Yet the woman who stood before them had to sacrifice her entire identity to reach that position. Queen Esther? They didn't even know her real name.

## Hadassah, the Girl Who Would Be Queen

Her given name was Hadassah, but she was known as Esther, an orphan raised by her cousin Mordecai. *Esther* and *Mordecai* were names that disguised their Jewish heritage. They were living in exile, far from their home and their native culture.

As the Persian Empire increased in dominance and expanded its borders, it trampled nations and people in its path. By 597 BCE, the Jews living in the southern kingdom (Judah) had been taken captive by the conquering Babylonians. They were sent into exile to what is now Iraq. The Jews lived as slaves in Babylon for approximately sixty years, when the Persian Empire conquered Babylonia. Now in power over the former Babylonian Empire,

Cyrus the Great, ruler of the Persian Empire, issued an edict allowing the Jews to return to Palestine.

Many Jews left to return to Jerusalem to rebuild the Temple, but many others stayed behind. Those who remained were not Babylonians, nor were they Persians. They were different, other. They were foreigners and regarded as insignificant. Cyrus the Great died in 486 BCE and Xerxes, one of his sons, became king. With the empire's change of rulers, Esther and Mordecai were swept into corridors of power in a way no one could have predicted.

King Xerxes ruled over 127 provinces that extended from India to Cush (Ethiopia). He was vain, decadent, and indulgent. He didn't lead by diplomacy; he ruled with power and the instruments of oppression and war. In his third year as king, he threw a lavish, seven-day party for his nobles, princes, military officers, and various other officials from across the empire.

At the party's seven-day mark, an intoxicated Xerxes summoned his wife, the beautiful Queen Vashti. She was ordered to appear before his guests to show off her beauty. But Vashti refused. It was unheard of for anyone—much less a woman—to disobey the king.

Some scholars interpret the text to say that Vashti was summoned to appear wearing nothing but her crown. Others suggest further that she may have been pregnant. At the very least, Vashti was not interested in being objectified in front of a crowd of drunken partygoers. So she refused the summons and Xerxes was publicly humiliated.

## STAYING TRUE TO YOUR IDENTITY
## CAN BE COSTLY

The dishonored king's response was swift. Xerxes's advisers recommended the king make an example of Vashti by banishing her permanently. Such drastic action would send a powerful warning throughout the empire. Even the queen could be easily replaced; men were the rulers of their households.

A few years passed and Xerxes began to pine for Vashti (see Esther 2:1). His attendants suggested a diversion in the form of a different woman. An empire-wide search was launched to identify the most beautiful virgins. Women were taken from their homes and families. The king spent the night with each one (and it wasn't for coffee and conversation). The selection process would end with his choosing a new queen. The runners-up remained in the king's harem.

Esther numbered among the abducted beauties.

The time she spent in the harem waiting for her night in the king's chambers turned out to be a period of transformation. Esther was treated with kindness by one of the eunuchs who took care of her. He gave her special beauty treatments, special food, and maids to attend her. No one knew her real name was Hadassah because Mordecai had told her to keep her nationality and family background a secret—an added layer of safety.

After twelve months of receiving special care, Esther's night arrived. There is no romance in this setting. Understand that she was powerless, stolen from her home, and ordered to appear before the king. Esther's history was kept secret, and any hopes for her future seemed useless. Esther existed to satisfy the king. Yet amid this horrific situation, Esther found favor. The king made her his queen. Xerxes held a banquet in Esther's honor, proclaiming an empire-wide holiday.

Vashti was gone. Hadassah was gone as well.

## Long Live Queen Esther

I find the book of Esther deeply troubling. A despotic king and his fawning enablers had, by royal decree, made life untenable for a generation of women and their families. Yet I am fascinated by Esther's journey of grace and favor amid a nightmare and all that it cost her.

Esther lost her name, Hadassah, and with it she lost her ethnic and religious identity. Even as the queen, she continued to hide her full self (see Esther 2:20). A strong drive to survive preserved her life, yet she paid a heavy price. She had to achieve the perfect representation of what her world wanted. I can't imagine she was the first woman who had to do that. I know from personal experience she wasn't the last.

Esther was a powerless woman. The example set by Vashti's banishment had shown what happened to women who attempted to use their own agency. There was protocol that dictated how women were allowed to be. Comply or face the consequences. Esther may have experienced favor, but she wasn't free. Not yet.

Many of us know what it feels like to hide our identity in

order to survive. We do what it takes to fit into our family, our workplace, our friendship group. We spend our energy trying to fit into our context, into society, into what is demanded of us according to someone else's terms.

## BEING DEVALUED FOR WHO YOU ARE

Elena was excited when she was offered an interview for a new position in her company. Reaching the interview stage affirmed her sense that she was a leader who had something to offer. She began to share some of her ideas in the interview when the interviewer, a new executive director, interrupted her.

"Elena, you're not seriously in the running for this position. To be honest, I don't even think you're the right person for the job you're in now. The only reason you're part of this team is because you're a wo–." He stopped himself, then got in even deeper. "Because you're eye candy. A lot of older men in the organization like to have you around the office."

Elena left the interview not knowing whom she could talk to. After this, whom could she trust? And now she knew that even her current job wasn't safe.

"You're eye candy." Her ideas and dreams were irrelevant. Her value to the organization had been made clear. She had nothing to offer other than her gender and her looks. Elena's skills, experience, and commitment to the organization were irrelevant. If she was going to fit, she would need to be perfectly pretty, pert, and popular. If she was to keep her job with this new director in charge, she needed to look attractive at all times to please the older men in the organization.

Elena lived this way for years. Her story is not unique. It's not even unusual.

I love musicals, and when I was a child, the movie *Grease* was one of my favorites. Set in a fifties high school, it told the love story of greaser Danny Zuko and sweet, preppy new girl Sandy Olsson. I was too young at the time to realize that Sandy transformed who she was and how she behaved to be with Danny. Danny changed a little, but nothing compared to Sandy. Sandy was already a great person, friendly and outgoing and a good citizen. But she felt she had to become someone else to fit in.

Your high school years might be far in the past. But how many times have you had to transform yourself to become a different person in order to earn approval or acceptance? You reinvented yourself to keep your job, hold onto a relationship, maintain your role in church, or simply to survive in your community.

Your efforts might have been rewarded with a promotion or a raise or recognition by the people in your community who "counted." But you weren't free. It's another broken identity that prevents you from living the life you were made for.

If we're honest with one another, it has been necessary at times to play along. Just for as long as we need to, then we'll change back to who we truly are. So as we comply in the interest of survival, we remain unaware of the cost to our identity and purpose. And it's the cost that will affect us for years to come.

## THE NIGHT OF THE TALK

It was a Sunday night and my mom's friends had dropped by. These women were my aunties, not because they were all blood relatives but as a mark of respect. We were Nigerians living far from home, and we all were part of one extended family. The women were preparing a huge steaming pot of stew that would form the base for our meals for the next few days. Chicken pieces were rubbed and seasoned; onions and hot peppers were sliced.

The smell of stew made me hungry and impatient. I'd visit the kitchen to charm a piece of chicken out of an aunty's hand and into my eager mouth. I grabbed what I could and returned to the living room where other women were sharing and storing food to take home. They talked, dissecting the events of life, telling about their children's accomplishments, sharing news from back home or catching each other up on the latest episode of *Dynasty*.

Sunday nights also were set aside for my hair to be combed through, greased with Dax Pomade or a SoftSheen product, and braided into cornrows. Once my enthusiasm for fresh cornrows wore off, about five minutes into the process, I became fidgety and bored. I would try to watch television or read a book. Then, with a sharp tug and a "Keep still or this will hurt you," my head would be pulled back in line. My aunts seemed to have forgotten something from their own cornrow days. Getting my thick Afro hair detangled, the comb through, the tight braids—it all hurt!

Still, those evenings were a rite of passage, a portal into the lives of these women. I would get to listen in on grown-up conversations when women were talking about love and life and work.

Late in the spring of 1981, the talk turned to Brixton, a section of London three miles from where we lived. It was the part of the city where we bought chicken and fish and the ingredients for stew. Sometimes my aunties and my mom bought lace or tights or cosmetics there. It was where we always saw someone we knew and, much to my annoyance, had to stop and talk for what seemed like hours.

In 1981 the rumbling pressure caused by poverty, high unemployment, recession, poor housing, racism, and escalating tensions—most notably between the police and young black citizens—erupted into rioting. Hundreds of people were injured in the clashes; shops and businesses were damaged, looted, or burned; and cars were set on fire. It was all over the news. At age seven I didn't understand much of what was happening. Yet when I watched the news coverage, I pieced together a fragmented picture that frightened me. They spoke of Brixton and its people, (of *us?*) in a way I didn't recognize. They didn't talk about people meeting and chatting in the market. They spoke of thugs, bad people, violence, and no-go zones. Were my family, my community, *bad people?*

In the summer of the same year, there were riots in other cities—Birmingham, Liverpool, Leeds. Each city had its own story, yet all the cities faced similar struggles—pain, poverty, and racial inequity.

When I eavesdropped on the adult voices at home, my aunties sounded frustrated and weary. I wanted to ask what it all meant,

but I could tell from the intensity in their voices that I shouldn't
ask. This was not children's talk; this was not even eavesdropping
talk.

I would lower my head and sit very still as my thick hair was
combed, greased, cornrowed. I closed my eyes and thought of
everything that helped me block out the pain of a sensitive scalp.
Only this time I tried to block out the fear in my sensitive heart
too. You and I both know that fear makes you feel powerless.

During one of these evenings, one voice rose above the others
to address me. It was my Aunty Bassey, my mom's most dear
friend and my favorite of all my beloved aunties. She spoke as
though she wasn't speaking only to me; she was speaking to a
generation of daughters on behalf of the women in the room.

Joannah, my dear, there's something you need to understand. Because you are black, you are going to have to
work hard at school. But it will not be enough to be good;
it will not be enough to be brilliant. You will have to be
better than everyone else. In addition, you are a woman.
That means you will have to work even harder than every
man there. So you understand, my dear, what this means
for you. You are black and you are a woman. You will have
to be at least twice as good. At least. It doesn't matter what
your friends are doing, what they are saying; you are not
them. It is different for you. You will have to be so good
that even if they do not like you for being black or they do
not respect you for being a woman, they will still employ
you because you are so clearly, far and above, the best at

what you do. My dear, you must work extra hard if you want to make it in this country.

Others murmured their agreement, then the conversation moved on.

## The Wounds Behind The Talk

I heard the same talk many more times from Aunty Bassey, from other aunties, and from my mom. It was rarely a bitter conversation. It was educational; it was medicinal. This was a generation of women that had left home, saying goodbye to families, in search of adventure and opportunity, in pursuit of their dreams and a better life. Life in return had given them the hard-earned, soul-stinging wisdom of experience.

They carried the scars of sacrifice on their callused hands. Long hours of hard work and study as they adjusted to another culture's weather, social conventions, and mind-sets. They endured misunderstanding, rejection, racism, and exclusion. Their skills, their education and intelligence, were regularly overlooked or discounted. They endured the indignity of slow, loud, patronizing questions about their choice of food, clothing, and music. They made sacrifices to remain in England even as others returned home to Nigeria. Not every marriage survived the adventure. Their beloved elders—the parents, aunties, and uncles they left behind—passed from this world to the next. And the women who had set out to find their way in another land had to let them go without being with them to say goodbye.

These women longed for home, but when they returned to visit, they found that the world they had left behind in Nigeria had changed. Their children, for whom they had given up everything, sometimes grew away from their heritage and culture. The next generation's Western ways bewildered the aunties who had raised their children right.

As I grew older, I began to imagine the women as they were when they were young. I tried to see their optimism, idealism, and wide-eyed innocence. It was there once; I was sure of that. It must have been there for these women, for how else were they brave enough to be pioneers and architects for the generation that they would carry in their own bodies?

Still, for all my aunties' accomplishment, commitment, wisdom, and hard work, they faced a powerlessness that was not easily overcome. The villains of poverty and injustice appeared to be winning. Equality remained a faint, distant dream that might never arrive. What could they do when they were powerless?

*The Talk,* given to virtually every black child I knew, was part of the solution. It was a strategy of hard truths shared to preempt the struggles our elders had faced. They wanted to steel us children by preparing us to fight, to work, to overcome, to achieve, and to prove ourselves. They wanted us to be tough enough to protect our vulnerability and deflect disappointments. We'd need to be fast, agile, disciplined, and strong. They wanted us to go farther than they had.

I was a black girl growing up in an unfair world that didn't always value me. I wouldn't hide my ethnicity even it if was an option. But thanks to The Talk, I had a plan. I didn't use it just for the successful career that my aunties told me to work toward. I took it further. I wanted more than a career; I wanted a successful life. I wasn't trying to compete with other people as much as I was fighting to prove my worth. I was competing against the forces that wanted to keep me powerless.

Ordinary was not enough. Extraordinary might buy me a second glance. I needed to do more. I needed to be more. There was only one option for a successful life. With or without the red leather boots, I'd need more than perfection. I'd need to be Wonder Woman.

## WILL YOU EVER LET WONDER WOMAN GO?

No matter where the feeling of powerlessness lingers, you want to believe you can bring out the red cape and red boots and fix it yourself. It seems we all have our version of morphing ourselves into a form of imposed perfection. We dedicate ourselves to becoming twice, even three times, as good. We behave in the "right" way and do whatever it takes—as defined by some outside authority. We exhaust ourselves to earn the recognition of people or systems and find that we have nothing left. We become our own version of Wonder Woman:

- The Wonder Woman Wife—perfectly pleasing in every way, even to critical mothers-in-law. She keeps the perfect home. She will be everything her man needs her to be and will ask nothing in return. It's fine. Really it is.
- The Wonder Woman Mother—keeping up with

sisters, friends, and church family. She can do it all
and be it all. Yes, she can organize the carpool. Yes,
she can organize gifts for Teacher Appreciation
Week. Yes, she will be PTA president. Of course, she
can volunteer at VBS this summer. And bake too.
Who doesn't love baking?

- The Wonder Woman Employee—gets things done,
high-achieving and ambitious, with limited emotional
response so as not to encumber male coworkers with
all that "feelings stuff." The definition of "feelings
stuff" includes having a hard day with a notoriously
difficult client that nobody else wants to deal with.
Or her stated need for decent maternity leave. In fact,
to prove that she's a good coworker, she'll work twice
as hard. Yes, she can stay for that inconvenient,
last-minute, late-night meeting that was not on the
schedule. It's just a part of the job. It's what it takes to
get noticed, even though they don't see her yet.

- The All-Purpose Wonder Woman—a physically
perfect specimen in every way: perky, tight all over,
with flawless skin and sparkling smile. She has an
up-to-the-second stylish look and is impressively fit,
follows a Paleo diet, plus Whole30, gluten-free,
organic, small-plate, clean-eating. A yoga-loving,
CrossFit-trained champion triathlete.

We think we must become Wonder Woman to reach crazy
ideals of perfection. Yet it's a lie to believe that Wonder Woman
was ever one woman in the first place.

The character of Wonder Woman (first encountered in comics) was created by noted psychologist Dr. William Moulton Marston. Inspired by early twentieth-century feminist thought, he stated, "Frankly, Wonder Woman is psychological propaganda for the new type of woman who, I believe, should rule the world." Alongside his ideals, he lived with two women, bearing children with both and living as a collective family. One of the women went out to work, the other raised all the children. Both were the key inspiration for Wonder Woman![1]

It's important to remember that Wonder Woman is entertainment, fiction developed from an amalgam of lofty ideals and complicated family relationships. I'll happily watch Wonder Woman in movies. I'll cheer when she helps the good guys and defeats the bad guys. Prude that I am, I'll probably still want to buy her a long Wonder sweater, but I'll always love her quest for justice and truth. And her red boots. Nonetheless, Wonder Woman is not a theological treatise on our God-given identity. She is not a description of God's Dream of You.

Would you be willing to let Wonder Woman go? Could you?

## REAL TALK

Life has taught us that our perfectionistic pursuits are necessary. If your mother-in-law doesn't approve of you, she will make life unbearable. Or you can choose to be eye candy at work, or join the ranks of the unemployed.

It took years before I even acknowledged my perfectionism. I didn't see it as overachievement. To me it seemed more like an essential tool for survival. If you're not prepared to be Wonder Woman, they won't even let you in the door. While this is a broken identity that we need to let go of, it's one that the world around us tends to reinforce. It's the broken identity that helps us land a job, keeps the peace (or a truce) in our homes, helps people accept and respect us (or a version of us anyway), and helps us climb the corporate ladder. In short, it helps us get by. Besides, how can you live the life you were made for when you are not given an opportunity to live it?

Can God redeem this? For an answer, let's return to the story of Esther and Mordecai. Haman, one of the king's noblemen, allowed a feud with Mordecai to push him into plotting evil. When Haman learned that Mordecai was a Jew, he resolved to kill all the Jews who remained in Xerxes's empire. He manipulated the king into creating an irrevocable law ordering that the Jews be killed (see Esther 3).

When Mordecai called on Esther to intercede for her people, at first she hesitated. Her new role in the royal court was to be beautiful and compliant. The king had not summoned her from the harem for a month—and she appeared only at the king's behest. To show up uninvited would endanger Esther's life. Vashti had been banished for a lesser offense.

When Esther indicated that she preferred to stick to her survival strategy, Mordecai gave his version of The Talk:

> Don't think for a moment that because you're in the palace you will escape when all other Jews are killed. If you keep quiet at a time like this, deliverance and relief for the Jews

will arise from some other place, but you and your relatives will die. Who knows if perhaps you were made queen for just such a time as this? (Esther 4:13–14)

Mordecai called on a powerless woman to exercise her power at a time when doing so could save the lives of an entire minority population. He called out Esther's identity in the face of an oppressive, male-dominated, pagan system. He reminded her that she was a Jew. He reminded her of her people's part in a bigger story—God's story. He even pointed to a bigger purpose. The lives of Esther's people living in exile needed to be protected.

In calling out Esther's identity, Mordecai called out her voice and her purpose. Esther, like you and me, needed to be reminded of who she was, not who she had become. If she remained passive, she would be complying with forces that held her captive to their definition of perfection. Look pretty, obey the men, and be silent. So this time Mordecai did not tell her to hide who she was. It was time to reveal her background and heritage. It was time to be Hadassah.

## ARE YOU READY TO RECOVER THE PERSON YOU TRULY ARE?

It was only when Esther embraced her full identity that she found her voice. She could finally speak as herself. This is when her purpose emerged and she recovered her spiritual authority. She called the Jews to fast. Then she approached the king without an invitation. When she brought her full identity to the king, her life and the lives of her people were saved and their enemy defeated. She still had the name Esther, but her identity, Hadassah, was back.

When we trade our identity for a perfectionistic alternative, even when it's for survival, it comes at a heavy cost. We lose our true selves and we lose our voices. We lose our spiritual authority, because perfectionism relies on our skills rather than God's power. It costs us our purpose because perfectionism has a different purpose than the one God has given us. We lose our courage, because at the root of perfectionism is fear.

God wants to redeem it all. Rather than your being transformed into a broken identity by the pressures of your world, He wants to transform you to recover who you fully are.

Are you ready to be led toward redemptive wholeness, even when you might still fear for your survival? It can be hard to imagine how God could lead us through that shift. But He is waiting for us, ready to lead us back to who we are.

> When we trade our identity for a perfectionistic alternative, even when it's for survival, it comes at a heavy cost. We lose our true selves and we lose our voices.

Of course, you play a big part in the process. Start with identifying the areas where you struggle with overachievement or perfectionism. Think through how you present yourself at work, at home, at church, in the community, and with friends. Take a careful look at each role you fill, and consider what it is costing you.

- Esther didn't face her crisis alone. She had a mentor who called out who she was and spoke to her purpose. We need people who will speak into our lives about who we have become. Who can you talk to?

- Esther recognized that, to take on the systems of the Persian Empire, she needed more than personal strength. Esther needed God, her stronger covenant Partner, to deliver her and her people. She called her entire community to fast and pray for three days. Our situations are bigger than we are. We need more than personal confidence, because we are engaged in a spiritual battle. We need to pray, fast, and gather others to join us. Who can you pray with?

- After all this preparation, Esther was ready. She faced the expectation of her culture, and instead of complying, she chose to speak up. She entered the king's presence knowing that doing so put her life at risk. Still, she spoke out against evil and saved a nation.

What would it look like to be who you truly are, to claim your real name and to reclaim your real voice? When you lose your identity in the perfectionism required to survive the world, it's painfully hard to find your way back. I was unaware that, in the process, I was losing my full God-given identity. I was unaware that I was losing my voice and my purpose.

As my voice began to emerge, it had battles of its own to face.

# The Day I Lost My Voice

H<small>EY</small>, G<small>IRL</small>,

I meet you often, in church and business, around the neighborhood. I meet you in every ethnicity and culture, and every class, and all made in the image of God. And when I meet you, I see the same thing, even though your journey to this moment is your own.

Your eyes tell me the most about you. It's all there: your passion, intensity, and excitement flicker. But uncertainty, fear, and even pain are present too. There's so much going on in you, you could burst!

You've got something to say, you've got a contribution to make. But it's a fight for you to speak about what burns in your heart.

When you speak, I hear the burden of your un-tapped potential, the fear of being overlooked. You are frustrated and weary, and your confidence is worn thin. As you talk, you dismiss and second-guess your vibrant ideas and insights. You qualify your dreams and goals (which are *brilliant*, by the way) with a resigned "I don't know." I look in those eyes and I can tell that you *do* know. But throwaway words create a shield, and you think they protect you. You are not alone in this.

It's the flickering flame in your eyes that helps me know that even though you have words, somewhere along the way you lost your voice. I want to tell you that I see you and hear you, but truthfully I don't think I fully see and hear you—not yet.

I don't know what happened that left you voiceless, but I'm glad you're searching to reclaim what was lost. The journey can be tough at times, but it has the power to ignite a flickering flame inside you.

Cheering you on,

Jo

ري

When I was ten years old, I loved to sing more than I loved to breathe. It was one of the few areas of my life that remained immune to outside influence. When I sang, I expressed myself freely. In other areas, I was working on perfection and trying to prove my value, but singing was different. When I sang I felt whole and free. It didn't matter if anyone was listening; when I sang, time and space were suspended, and I was lost in the moment. A moment that felt pure and innocent. A moment where I simply felt like I was being me.

Nothing else could set me free like singing did.

When the choir at my school was preparing to perform in front of the student body, I was invited to perform my first solo. I was thrilled. To be ten and singing in front of the entire school! I memorized my part and practiced every day. When the day arrived, I wore a brightly colored summer dress, my favorite.

My music teacher started playing the melody on the piano and nodded at me to join her. Excitement and adrenalin stole my lines at first. My voice wavered, straining for an opportunity to be heard. I closed my eyes and allowed my voice to outmaneuver its competitors—and it came out. It was my voice, my unexpectedly adult voice.

I sang every word.

*Who will buy this wonderful morning?*
*Such a sky you never did see!*[1]

I opened my eyes when I was done, and one of my teachers was teary. For weeks after the applause had died down, my teachers told one another, and me, that I had a gift, a wonderful voice. They urged me to keep singing, urged me to share my gift with others.

Their affirmation was encouraging and inspiring. Their words gave me confidence, and I committed to stay in the choir for another year. Perhaps I did have a gift that I could enjoy with others. If only the voices of the teachers, the voices that spoke with authority and clarity, would come along with me to the playground. Unfortunately, my teachers weren't there.

There were two girls in the grade above me, the kind of best friends who eventually hated each other. Carol was tall, thin, and outspoken. She seemed so much older than the rest of us. She was only eleven, but she was so worldly wise compared to the rest of us that she seemed like a fourteen-year-old. She even dressed much older than the rest of us.

She told us she knew Michael Jackson, that they were friends, and she tearfully made us sign a large, pink "Get Well Soon" card after he got burned in the making of a Pepsi video. She told us that he was really hurt, but that when they talked he said he was scared but would be all right.

It never occurred to any of us that she wasn't telling the truth. At least it hadn't occurred to me.

Veronica was sporty and popular. She was pretty and had beautiful hair. She didn't style her hair in cornrows like the rest of us. She had long, thick pigtails that were naturally soft and shiny. She wore nice clothes, all the time.

The other thing to note about Carol and Veronica: they ruled the playground. It just so happened that on the day I sang with the school choir, they decided that I would be their latest subject of attention. Unfortunately.

"Oh, Joannah, you sound like an opera singer," Carol said. Then she laughed, smirking and turning toward Veronica in that way only tween girls can do. It wasn't meant as a compliment. Veronica burst out laughing. Then they slowly looked me up and down, showing their disapproval.

"And where did you get that dress?"

I began to respond, not realizing they weren't interested in the answer. I mentioned that this dress was a special gift from my mom, and she loved it when I wore dresses. They looked at each other and laughed. Then they turned away, dismissing me. They were done with me . . . for now.

And so it began. Every day there was a comment, something sarcastic or a direct criticism of my clothing. Or it was a comment about my face or my hair, about my personality, about my singing. Or they'd stop talking as I walked by. Sometimes I got a look, followed by laughter.

I tried walking to school by a different route and leaving home at a different time to avoid them. I would look down and walk slowly or run quickly to avoid them. Yet there was one place I could never avoid them—the playground.

It wasn't long before they enlisted others. They befriended girls and guys from my grade, kids who felt loved by the acceptance of the big girls. Every day when I was mocked, the kids who had been befriended would stand in silent pity. At times, they would laugh awkwardly. I made a mental note of the ones who laughed a little too enthusiastically. Of course, none of the teachers knew what was going on. These girls were sweetness and light when teachers were around. In a pre-Internet era, they found a way to tweet their disgust with a whisper, to let me know I wasn't Pinterest perfect. They text messaged me their disgust with a derisive glance.

Maybe there was something wrong with me. Maybe my voice was weird.

I prayed that God would make it stop. Make them stop being so cruel and have them just leave me alone. To my great relief, a few weeks later Carol and Veronica fell out over some other drama. I thought, finally, the daily bullying would end. Then I was horrified when they became friends again the following week. Best friends.

I felt I had to confront them.

"What did I ever do to you?"

"Joannah, why can't you take a joke? We don't make fun of you."

"Yes, you always make fun of me. You bully me every day! What I wear, what I do, what grades I get, how I talk. Every day, everything I do. You *do* make fun of me."

"You just can't take a joke. What's wrong with you?"

I told my lunchtime supervisor about the bullying. She believed me, which was a relief, but my heart sank when she told me to "just ignore them." It was much too late for that. I wasn't strong enough for that.

Every mocking statement from Carol and Veronica was more powerful than a mere kick or a slap. Their words delivered daily wounds, bruising me deeply. Who did I think I was, anyway? Thinking I had a voice, that I had a gift? I couldn't fight back; they said in public the things I privately feared were true. My shameful secret was out: I wasn't good enough. And now everyone could see it.

Even *if* I could sing, I was a nothing and a nobody. I didn't have Carol's style or connections. I wasn't pretty like Veronica. Everybody liked them; everybody pitied me. I was forgettable, temporary. And it made me feel vulnerable and small.

The bullying eventually stopped, but not because of an intervention or because I told anyone. It stopped when the school year ended. However, that year changed me in lasting ways. I decided to start acting differently. Innocence was for the bullied. I would not be small again; I would not be vulnerable. I was someone else now: wiser, stronger, and tougher. And I never wore that dress again.

I brooded over the friends who had watched and laughed

while I was bullied. I wouldn't forget them. I wouldn't trust so easily next time. There were even times I treated them the way I'd been treated, just so they could know how it felt. Now I was the bully.

I felt stronger, but I didn't realize I was weaker than ever. My wounded heart was infected with bitterness, my mind scarred by bullying words. Life moved on, but I hadn't healed.

I still don't understand why I was bullied that year. Sometimes being chosen as the object of derision doesn't have a weepy backstory, and in the end the reason why didn't matter. What mattered most was that the bullies were successful. Though singing had been life giving to me, it wasn't worth the rejection and pain. I'd been mocked daily for the entire school year over the way I sang. Why would I stand in front of people and sing again? I knew better now. I left the school choir. I found other, more acceptable interests that endeared me to life on the playground.

That's the year I lost my voice.

## How We Lose Our Voices

When we refer to losing our voice, we might be talking about how we sound when we have a bad cold or laryngitis. More often when we talk about our voice, we're referring to something deeper and more purposeful. When we talk about our voice, we mean our most authentic self. We're talking about the real us—not hidden but expressed in the world around us. Our voice captures our passions, our values, our gifts and talents. Our voice is our identity in action, making its unique contribution in the world.

The English word *voice* comes from the Latin root word voc- or vox, the same root from which we get the word *vocation*. Most importantly, our sense of purpose and vocation is an integral part of our God-given design. From the beginning, God's people had a twofold purpose: to know God intimately, but also to represent Him in the world. The people of God were given a commission to bear spiritual fruit. They were given the responsibility to live as a blessing to the world (see Genesis 1:28–31). Throughout biblical history, this commission would continue. God's people were to be a light to the nations. Their lives were to illustrate what knowing God looked like through their relationships and actions.

When Jesus invited people into relationship, He also invited them to contribute alongside Him. Writing to the Ephesian Christians, Paul made it clear they would find their identity in Christ. In Christ they would discover who they were as well as what they were living for (their voices, their vocations). God's gracious, life-transforming redemption reaches as far as redeeming a person's purpose.

God redeems our voices. He gives us a new song.

I've noticed that many women downplay their passion and gifts. Sometimes it's out of shyness or embarrassment. Yet more often they feel insecurity that grows out of past experiences. At times, women apologize for who they are. They minimize their abilities, as if they're expecting someone to tell them they're arrogant for having talent, ability, and dreams. Some women, particularly those who reach high levels of influence in their field, are plagued by what is known as Imposter Syndrome,[2] or the impostor experience. Even though they're highly accomplished, they are overwhelmed by self-doubt and worry that they're about to be exposed and lose their jobs. Oscar winner Lupita Nyong'o said, "I go through [acute impostor syndrome] with every role. I think winning an Oscar may in fact have made it worse."[3]

How can brilliant, beautiful, strong, gifted, accomplished women grow silent? I have to wonder how many of them had been shaken up by an encounter on the playground.

What is your playground experience, the one that never left you even though you left grade school years ago? You and I know the playground isn't limited to our elementary-school years; it extends to every chapter of our lives. And so do the bullies. They steal our peace of mind, our joy, and our confidence.

Melinda loved inviting people into her home. Having people know they were welcome was a gift to her. Many of her friendships were formed over conversations in the kitchen. Eager to make friends in her new church, she offered her home for a new Bible study group. She was excited—until Donna and Jill's thinly veiled, yet loudly voiced, criticisms began to eat away at her. It was the same every week: comments about her cooking, her furniture and her style, her hosting. Now she felt tense and nervous every week. Occasionally she made up an excuse, saying one of her children had taken sick, just to keep people from coming over.

She couldn't bear to see the smirks and knowing looks as Donna and Jill confided their distain. If they intended to make her feel bad, it was working. The next time a Bible study group was being formed, Melinda would choose not to offer her home as the meeting place. She wasn't planning on participating either.

Melinda's voice of welcoming hospitality and providing a place for study had been silenced.

Marci didn't lose her voice; it was stolen. When she shared her ideas and strategies with a colleague, she didn't expect the colleague to present them as her own at the next team meeting. When it came Marci's turn to contribute, she was left with nothing to say because her idea was stolen from her. The team adopted Marci's plan, as presented by the colleague, and it was successful. But she never got the recognition for her contribution, and she overhead her boss express concern about Marci's "lack of passion and initiative."

Kiki's voice was broken. She always wanted a large family in a big, rambling house. Now she was shattered, living in the ruins of a painful marriage, amid the wreckage caused by the words and actions of an emotionally abusive former husband. This is not how she hoped to raise her children. And even though she knew she was a good mother and a good woman, her ex's words had taken away her confidence. He made her feel small. Now Kiki constantly questioned her skills and her decision making. She could hear the cruel words of her ex, even when she was alone in the darkness, fighting to fall asleep.

When did you lose your voice? Pause now to think how it happened and by whose agency.

When our voices have been taken, we redirect our lives toward "more acceptable" interests. We excuse the damage caused by having been silenced by saying we are only being realistic. We downplay our gifts and subdue our talents. And instead of the life we were designed for, we live the life we think we can get away with.

Or more accurately, the life we feel can avoid more silencing. We call it safe, but in reality it's a denial of who we are. When we go along with this, we are party to the silencing of ourselves.

We change our identities. We make ourselves small.

## DOES THE BULLYING EVER END?

Centuries after Joseph lived in Egypt, the reigning pharaoh enacted a policy that ensured the Hebrews would be enslaved and brutalized (see Exodus 1:11–14). Later he commanded that every newborn Hebrew boy be killed immediately. The Hebrews suffered for years under oppressive Egyptian regimes until God called Moses to free the people from bondage in Egypt.

Moses stood up to Pharaoh, and eventually the people of God left their land of enslavement. The Exodus was followed by forty years spent wandering in the desert. But finally, the Hebrews arrived at the Jordan River, across which they could see the land God had promised them.

Moses passed the torch to Joshua, who led the people to conquer and occupy their new homeland. After Joshua and his generation of leaders died (see Judges 1), the Israelites continued to battle invaders from neighboring tribes. By the time Deborah emerged as a judge (leader) of Israel, the people had been oppressed for twenty years by Jabin, a Canaanite king with an army so brutal the Israelites had abandoned the roads to seek safety (see Judges 5:6).

The people asked for a king, and God gave them Saul, who was followed by David, the greatest king of Israel. Under David's leadership, Israel defeated its enemies and the people lived in peace. The golden era was short lived, however. After David's son and replacement, King Solomon, died, the nation split into two kingdoms.

Within three hundred years, after generations of kings had assumed power and then left the scene, both kingdoms (Judah and Israel) were conquered. The people who survived were sent into exile, where once again they were powerless in the hands of a victorious superpower.

We know the names of some of these evil Gentile leaders. Nebuchadnezzar plays a starring role in the book of Daniel, and Haman sought to annihilate the Jews in the book of Esther.

In the four gospels that begin the New Testament, God's people were living in the region that God had given them hundreds of years before, but now it was occupied by Rome. The history of the people of God is littered with bullies. Egypt, then neighboring Gentile tribes, followed by distant world superpowers to the east, and then, by the first century of the Common Era, the Roman Empire had crushed the souls of the Israelites.

## NOT FORGOTTEN

Yet in the wake of all this suffering, we see God's redeeming power at work. God not only rescued His people again and again, but also redeemed their purpose and restored their voices.

- When Pharaoh ordered the deaths of every Hebrew newborn boy, the Hebrew midwives risked their own lives by protecting the baby boys (see Exodus 1:17–19).

- Joshua faced his fears and led the people to occupy the Promised Land in the face of their enemies.
- Judges of Israel, such as Ehud, Deborah, and Gideon, routed oppressors and brought peace.
- Kings David and Solomon kept the nation's enemies at bay.
- The victories (and redemption) achieved by Moses and Deborah were given voice in songs (see Exodus 15; Judges 5). The warrior-king David was also a poet and a musician. He voiced his victories, pleas, celebrations, and imprecations in a collection of songs, the book of Psalms. God's redemption meant God restored the voices of His people.
- Even when God's people were exiled and enslaved, God moved to redeem them through unlikely figures. Cyrus the king of Persia gave Jewish exiles the freedom to return to Jerusalem (see Ezra 1). Nehemiah, a mere cupbearer, was charged to rebuild the city's wall (see Nehemiah 1 and 2).
- The prophets risked death to tell the people about God's promise of One who would come in the future to break the yoke of oppression and to bring justice and peace (see Isaiah 9). They spoke of Israel's redeemed purpose as a light to the Gentile nations (see Isaiah 49:6). God used the voices of the prophets to keep reminding the people of the life they were made for.

## God Sees You

Yet the significance of these stories might get lost if you feel small and silenced. What I have recounted here covers eras of history, not just a few generations. God used mass migrations of people, an astounding variety of leaders (both righteous and evil), the voices of prophets, and much more to set the stage for the coming of Jesus the Messiah. When I think about the bullying I endured in grade school, it seems almost trivial by comparison.

But it is never trivial when the voice of any child of God is silenced. Long before the pharaohs of Egypt, the kings of Israel and Judah, and the prophets of God, a vulnerable and marginalized woman used her voice to accept a promise from God that she hardly dared believe could be true.

God spoke a promise to an aged couple named Abram and Sarai. He would take away Sarai's disgrace in the community by giving her and her husband a son. God promised that their son would be the father of a lineage numbering more than the stars in the sky. Sarai had been infertile even before she passed her child-bearing years; God's promise was difficult to accept. All they could do was wait for the day to come.

Days became months, then years. Nothing happened. Sarai decided to take matters into her own hands. She gave her Egyptian servant Hagar to Abram as a wife, in order to produce the heir God had claimed would be born. Hagar had no alternative but to go along with the scheme. She became pregnant and Abram finally had a child. Hagar, perhaps buoyed by her newfound status, began to disrespect her mistress, Sarai. Sarai complained to Abram and his passive response permitted Sarai to deal with Hagar as she pleased.

It was not Sarai's finest hour. She treated Hagar so harshly that the woman ran away into the wilderness, risking both her life and her child's. She escaped Sarai's harsh treatment, but the wilderness held little hope of anything better.

An angel of the Lord met Hagar and instructed her to return home, even though her return would be temporary and inevitably difficult. He also comforted her and told her who her child would become. She may have been powerless, caught up in someone else's broken story, but God's redemptive hand was still at work. She returned to Sarai and Abram, and her son Ishmael was born. In response to the angel encounter, Hagar used a name for God, El-roi, saying, "You are the God who sees me" (Genesis 16:13).

The name El-roi communicates not only God's awareness but also His interest. It communicates that in seeing Hagar, God also was with her. He heard her, understood her, and helped her. Hagar's voice mattered to God. Finally, she was more than a slave, more than a womb. She was important, valuable, validated by God.

God sees who you are, who you *fully* are.
He sees your story, He sees the life you can
bring, and He sees your potential and
purpose. He knows and hears your voice.

"You are the God who sees me." There is Hagar's voice. Who would have thought a powerless woman at the end of herself would be able to give the God of the universe a name? Stop and think about that. An Egyptian slave, a woman in a culture where women were little more than property even under the best of circumstances, gave God a name!

What a reminder that God sees who you are, who you *fully* are. He sees your story, He sees the life you can bring, and He sees your potential and purpose. He knows and hears your voice.

## PUTTING OUR VOICES TO USE

Decades have passed since I walked around that school playground. I want you to know that in the years that followed, I found a way to recover my voice. I found the courage to sing. Later I found the courage to speak in front of people and to discover my *vocare,* my vocation. It didn't happen in isolation; I learned to hear the encouragement of good friends, supportive family, wise teachers and mentors, and to finally believe them.

Nonetheless, the thing that changed me most was discovering more about the nature of the God who saw me and knew me. I expected a distant being whose love and attention I had to earn. Someone I'd have to prove myself to. Instead, I encountered a covenant Partner who saw my broken identity and made me new. I learned that this God was also a Father. It was a revelation that shattered my worldview, and to this day it continues to transform me from the inside out.

Have you lost your voice? Not just the words you use, but your full, God-breathed identity? Do you feel like an impostor waiting to be exposed and humiliated?

Have you been silenced in your passions and purpose, in what you are living for? Have you lost your *vocare,* your voice and your vocation?

Were your dreams for glorious living crushed by bullies who silenced the person you were designed to be?

You might even have pressed the mute button on the voice you were given and the life you were made for. In running away from the pain, did you enter the wilderness where you allowed your dreams to die?

No matter the damage done to you, no matter the running and hiding, this truth remains in force: God sees you. Did you hear? God sees you. He *sees* you. God turns His eyes and fills His eyes with *you.*

GOD. SEES. YOU.

The God who sees you is worth knowing. He has the power to redeem your voice and give you a new song.

Ask Him to restore your voice.

# God's Child

Dear You,

I can tell that you feel you should be past this by now. That you should be bolder, stronger—or pick some other archetype of an empowered kind of woman. Instead, you feel rejected and insecure. You have your reasons, your people, your experiences that left you this way.

What you hate most is the way this seems to seep into everything. The way your need for acceptance and approval have gone beyond a longing to a way of life. You have morphed into so many things that other people need you to be, you don't know who you are anymore. Losing your identity because you wanted to be loved turned out to be a poor trade.

The guilt deepens when you think of your faith in the mix of all this. Could God ever be pleased with you when you act like this, considering all that He has done? Sure, He loves you, but does He like you? Does He approve of you?

Yes, love. Absolutely, unequivocally yes. Read on.

Jo

☙

became a Christian at a Methodist church when I was nine years old. A school friend invited me along to one of the youth events, where I was told enthusiastically about Jesus. He was a Friend, a Brother, and a Savior. He sounded amazing.

It wasn't long before I committed my life to Him. I loved hearing more about Him, about His followers changing the world. That sounded like a dream come true, and I wanted to be involved. We read the Bible and we learned about prayer, about worship. We learned about the power of the Holy Spirit. I devoured everything I was taught. I wanted to know as much as possible about God.

But when they told me God was a father, it didn't quite register. Not because I didn't believe it was true. It was that I didn't understand what that truth meant or what it was supposed to look like. I heard sermons and songs about the love of God the Father. They spoke of God's attention and devotion. They painted a picture of a merciful, loving Father actively involved in our lives, expressing His love, moving on our behalf. My father hadn't been involved in my life beyond a few letters across the continents. I didn't want to be disrespectful, but God the Father didn't make any sense at all. So I focused on who Jesus was and carried on.

As I grew older, a picture of God did begin to emerge, but it wasn't positive. God was a father, but He was distant, removed. Disinterested, even. I felt that I would have to do a lot to make Him notice me. I couldn't expect Him to provide; I couldn't expect Him to be there for me. He had other priorities, other children. I'd need to work hard, twice as hard to earn His approval; I'd have to do something extra special to win His affection.

My broken filters were creating an inaccurate picture of God, which in turn affected how I related to Him. I saw plenty of healthy father-daughter relationships around me, but they weren't real to me. I knew it was possible for a father to be good, wonderful even. I just wasn't sure a father would want to love *me*. I certainly didn't think God would. I had no personal frame of reference for an active, involved father-daughter relationship. I didn't realize it at the time, but my experience, or lack thereof, was shaping my theology. And not in a good way.

I knew I belonged to God, but my understanding was that this was conditional. I needed to know my place and stay there. I was to be obedient; I was to serve; I was to be grateful for Jesus. Plus, I was to rely on the Holy Spirit. God would be disappointed with anything less.

## Fresh Insights into Ancient Truths

As Christians in the early church shared the gospel, they began to reach people who weren't Jews. Those who traveled to other regions to preach the gospel were witnesses, leaving areas where they were known to cross cultures and continents. Jesus gave His followers this commission, and the early centuries of the Common Era saw the message spread through the known world as Christians accepted their mission. They went into Gentile areas, where people had their own stories and their own heritage. Jacob, Joseph, Deborah, Esther, and other heroes of the Jews were not known in the Gentile stories. The significance of God's covenants forged with Abraham and Sarah, Moses and David weren't part of the Gentile stories. Yet in telling the story of God, the first Christians needed to find a way to explain the difference Jesus makes in a person's life.

To the Jews who believed, Jesus was the promised Messiah who had been talked about and anticipated for hundreds of years. But for Gentiles, the idea of a Messiah was a foreign concept. Still, a decision was needed. The act of faith—to a Jew or to a Gentile—was a decision to follow a different leader, to love and obey Jesus. They weren't simply making a decision about adopting a new belief system. They weren't exchanging the Temple of Diana or the Temple of Apollo for the King who would live within them, making each of them the temple of God.

Nor were they deciding to try hard to do the right things in pursuit of a new god. Instead, they would discover the fullness of a God who through the Cross had reached to them even though they were far away. This is the God who brought them close, considering them His very own.

Paul took the gospel to Rome and to Asia Minor (modern-day Turkey). He was imprisoned more than once; he was beaten, whipped, stoned, and shipwrecked (see 2 Corinthians 11:24–28). He went to the most pagan cities in the world, centers of worship to pagan gods and goddesses. These were centers of spiritual darkness, where he preached Jesus. All this from a man who, before his life-changing encounter with Jesus, spent his time hunting down followers of Jesus (see Acts 22:3–5). But after a blinding experience during which Jesus spoke to him, this well-studied man's eyes were opened to the new story of God's redemption.

So years later, when Paul spoke to Gentile believers about the transformative nature of life with Jesus, he chose illustrations from their world that would communicate the weight of biblical truths. Scholars note that a large portion of the Roman Empire was enslaved, possibly due to the Roman tendency to enslave rather than kill those they conquered.[1] Furthermore, large numbers of people lived as indentured servants. It seems that those who weren't enslaved owned slaves.

Paul was determined to show Gentile believers that belonging to God and being given a new identity was not the same as the servitude so many lived under. Their servitude was defined by fear. But being God's servants didn't mean they were property; rather it meant that they had a new identity in relationship with the Creator of the universe.

## ADOPTION: A PICTURE OF THE NEW COVENANT

When Paul wrote to church communities about God's redeeming power, he often illustrated his point with an idea that was familiar to those living in Greco-Roman culture. He drew on a common understanding of adoption to give Gentile Christians an illustration of their covenant relationship with God.

> So you have not received a spirit that makes you fearful slaves. Instead, you received God's Spirit when he adopted you as his own children. Now we call him, "Abba, Father." (Romans 8:15)

> But when the right time came, God sent his Son, born of a woman, subject to the law. God sent him to buy freedom

for us who were slaves to the law, so that he could adopt us
as his very own children. (Galatians 4:4–5)

Long before he laid down earth's foundations, he had us
in mind, had settled on us as the focus of his love, to be
made whole and holy by his love. Long, long ago he
decided to adopt us into his family through Jesus Christ.
(What pleasure he took in planning this!) (Ephesians
1:4–5, MSG)

Adoption was a common practice in the Greco-Roman world.
It usually happened when a Roman citizen who had no male heir
would choose someone, often a slave, to receive the inheritance
and continue the family legacy.

When a slave was adopted in this way, the former slave's entire
world was changed. The adoption was marked by a ceremony.
The person who now was a son signed papers stating that he re-
nounced all connection to his old life and family. His debts were
written off. The signed papers meant that the new father by adoption had complete control over every part of his son's life. He also
had to look after his son. Furthermore, while the father could
disown a biological son, an adopted child could never be disowned. And when the father died, the adopted son received his
inheritance and continued his father's legacy.

Gentile Christian congregations in Rome, Galatia, and Ephesus knew that adoption redeemed a person's life, restoring an identity that had been stolen by slavery. They understood that adoption
meant that instead of living under an owner, a person received a

father and a family. They understood that they now had a future
and an inheritance from God.

> If we are going to embrace our full identities,
> know our names, and live out our vocations as
> we speak with our true voices; if we are going
> to embrace who we are and what we're living
> for, we need to know *whose* we are.

God Himself had adopted them. And whether they were rich
or poor, male or female, Jew or Gentile, slave or free, New Testament believers knew who they were and what they were living for.
They were chosen and redeemed by God, through Jesus.

If we are going to embrace our full identities, know our
names, and live out our vocations as we speak with our true voices,
if we are going to embrace who we are and what we're living for,
we need to know *whose* we are. We need to understand personally
and authentically what it means that we belong to God by
adoption.

## Knowing the God Who Redeems You

Like believers who were part of the early church, we need the revelation that we are God's children and that He's our Father. Furthermore, we need to know what kind of father He is.

He's the Father who delighted to choose us as His children,
and He will never abandon or reject us. And from that loving
foundation, with our permanent status as adopted children, a new

identity and inheritance is given to us. We can spend our lives discovering all that our Father has for us and gloriously live into it. It's good news, yet completely counter to a worldview that distorts our identities and silences our voices based on *oughts* and *shoulds* defined by the world around us. We already are worthy without our doing one thing to earn it. It's almost too good to be true, but it is true!

For some of us whose experience of knowing an earthly father has been painful or complex, the idea of God being a good father can be a bewildering concept. My experiences overrode the truths that Paul wrote about, describing God as our Father. I desperately needed a reintroduction to who God was and who I was in God's eyes. I needed to be told whom I belonged to.

## I WANT MY DADDY

It was a hot summer Sunday evening in London, 1990. I was sixteen years old and on my way to church. It wasn't the church I usually attended. I loved the people there, but as I got older and entered high school, it felt a little too traditional for me. The church had declined in size and my friends had left for other churches or left the church completely. I wanted to meet Christians my own age to be friends with.

There was another church nearby that was known for more contemporary expressions of worship and teaching that were more engaging. Most importantly, on Sunday evenings it was teeming with teenagers and young adults. I even saw some school friends there. (I had no idea they were Christians, and I think they felt

the same about me!) For a church in London in the nineties to
have so many teenagers and young adults in attendance had to be
something special. That said, this high schooler had another
reason for attending: the drummer was very, *very* good looking.
We'd never spoken, but I knew that I was his destiny. We just
needed an opportunity to run into each other. He just needed
to see me, to look into my eyes, and the rest would be . . . a
testimony.

That's when Operation Destiny's Child was born.

My preparation was meticulous. The church would be packed
full of people that night, so I needed to ensure that the worship-
band drummer would see me. I had to make myself visible. I selected an outfit appropriate to make me . . . unforgettably visible.
Based on the length of the "skirt" (belt?) I wore, many would say
it wasn't appropriate.

Next step: makeup. I wasn't good at selecting colors or applying cosmetics (these were the days before I encountered MAC,
and once you go MAC you don't go back), but I was enthusias-
tic. I put on a lot of mascara to accentuate my eyes, which I felt
were my finest combination feature and weapon. I found an or-
ange lipstick or lip gloss and applied it with liberal vigor. Why
leave things only to my eyes?

I brought a friend with me for backup. When we arrived I
didn't want to seem desperate by sitting in the front row, so we sat
in the second row. I was in the drummer's direct line of view. Ex-
cellent. The plan for Operation Destiny's Child was as follows. As
soon as the meeting was ending, I would run up to the stage and
offer to help him pack up his drum kit. When he looked at me,

seeing me for the first time, he'd be dazzled by my beauty and our scintillating conversation. At that moment he would *know*. And we would have a testimony.

My plan was flawless.

The church service began and the worship was amazing, especially the percussion! I sang as loudly as I could and danced passionately, just so the drummer would know I was no part-timer. I was a committed believer with a heart for worship. The teaching portion of the service seemed to take forever. But I could handle it. I was prepared to contend for my miracle.

Finally, the service was ending. It was time, and I was ready. I was *born* ready. Then just as Operation Destiny's Child was about to commence, a woman stepped forward and spoke (I tried not to resent the way she was interrupting the course of love). She held forth:

> As we prayed before tonight's meeting, a number of us
> sensed God was pointing out a specific situation for a
> member of the congregation. There's a young woman here
> who doesn't know that God is her Father. She'd never
> known her earthly father, and she feels like an orphan.
> She's always felt like this. But God wants her to know that
> He knows her and sees her and that He is her Daddy. If
> that is you, then please come forward at the end because a
> member of our prayer team would love to pray with you.

I heard the sound of a young woman crying. Her broken voice was saying, "I want my Daddy. I want my Daddy." Then it changed to "I want a Daddy. I want a Daddy." Then I realized that that young woman was me.

I didn't feel exposed or humiliated; it made perfect sense that when a group of people asked God if He wanted to say something, He would tell them. That type of thing happened regularly at that church. I just never expected that God had anything to say to me.

In that moment I was revealed. My deepest self, my longings, my fears, my grief. All of it was brought out into the open. I discovered that God cared for me—for minority, voiceless me. More than that, He wanted to step in and father me. For years I'd refused to cry about the past. It was not so much an act of defiance; just because I felt like crying about it would never change anything.

However, that night I had no time to feel self-protective. The anguish that I had tried to silence erupted. There may have been up to four hundred people in the sanctuary that night. Yet in that moment, it was God seeing me, God meeting *me*. All of me. Time stood still as I shook and wept and wailed for my wasted years.

Even at that, there still was the matter that this was happening during the worship service and four hundred people were trying to have a spiritual moment of their own. Everyone had been interrupted by wailing from the young woman in the second row.

Members of the worship band had been asked by their leader to "gently cover what is happening." That meant "drown it out." There were two problems as they began to play. They played tender songs about God's love, which in that moment only made me cry harder. So they increased their volume, and being the competitive person I am, I got louder too. At one point I was shouting, "I want a Daddy!" at top volume.

Eventually I (well, everyone) was rescued when two sweet ladies from the prayer team gently but firmly guided me to another room to get me some help. They knew the congregation needed relief.

There I met the pastor and his wife. I was struck by the kindness in their eyes. I immediately knew they didn't judge me, and perhaps because I didn't know them, when they asked me to tell my story, I told them everything.

I told these loving strangers about my father's absence, about foster care, about the confusion I felt. I told them I didn't know who I was, and while I loved Jesus, I couldn't get head or heart around God as a father. *Father* was just a word to describe someone who went away, leaving me behind. I didn't know that God actually loved me. I wasn't sure that I believed it, and I didn't know how to believe it. (I wasn't going to lie to these people.) They listened and then prayed for me. As they prayed I felt as though a warm blanket had wrapped itself around me. That was the first day I felt at peace.

"I still don't get it," I said. "I still don't get how all of this changes anything."

The pastor smiled. "The great thing about God being your Father, Joannah, is that you don't have to get it. It's His responsibility to get it through to you."

When I met my girlfriend in the sanctuary, I looked like a hot mess, and when I say "hot," I mean sweaty. My clothes were crumpled. My heavily applied mascara and weird lipstick now were spread across my face and chin. I clutched my used tissues. The drummer boy did not call me, no surprise.

But as my friend and I walked into the summer night, I realized my destiny had changed. God saw me and reached out to me.
The past did not have to define me. I was His. I was His child.
And though I didn't understand it yet, I knew it would change
everything. As the haze left behind by an hour spent sobbing wore
off, it gave way to another unfamiliar feeling. Hope.

## Your Father Will Give You Peace

You've been adopted into God's family. His choice of you for
adoption is permanent; you will never be disowned or rejected.

Your past—old names, old debts, old story, old history—is
not only old but it's over. He has paid the full price. In your former
life, you may have been owned by destructive patterns and relationships, by hurts, habits, and hang-ups, by the insecurity of
finding your way in the world. But now you are fathered. The
things that once defined you don't have to shape you forever. He
transforms your entire life.

That summer night in London was not the culmination of an
identity shift; it was the small, weepy, broken beginning of redemption. That night I got a glimpse of my Father's glory. When
we think of glory, we might think of drama and majesty, un-
equalled might and victory. Yet glory in the Bible also refers to the
weightiness of God, the substance of God, the felt presence of
God.

But perhaps like me you just don't get any of it.

You know you're meant to believe that God is a good Father,
but your experiences of fatherhood have damaged you. You carry

them into your prayer life, your Bible study, your giving, your successes and failures. You carry those experiences everywhere, and they don't stop with your relationship with God. You feel stuck and you don't know how to change it.

Or it may be that leadership in the church or authority figures in government, in politics, and in other earthly realms have distorted your picture of those in power. And with these experiences informing your current understanding, you're afraid of God and His getting close to you.

If this or if any part of it describes you, then a redeemed life sounds more like cruel poetic fantasy than reality. Fortunately, it is not your job to manufacture peace and hope. It's not even your responsibility to understand God. It is God's joy to get it through to you. God is willing and able to redeem every part of your life, even your picture of Him. Are you willing to discover who God the Father really is?

Pause to reflect on your relationship with God as Father. How do you feel about what God feels about you?

How do you feel about God in general, and in particular God as your Father? (It's important to be honest.)

Take time to reflect on the experiences that have shaped your view of God the Father. If you had positive experiences, is there anyone you want to thank? If so, how can you celebrate that person?

For those with negative experiences, what can you do to heal from the difficult experiences? Remember, God doesn't need you to do that so you will be able to like Him more. He just wants you to be healed and whole, period.

For a closer look at the nature and character of God, explore Luke 15 and the person of Jesus, because "the Son radiates God's own glory and expresses the very character of God, and he sustains everything by the mighty power of his command" (Hebrews 1:3).

# Known and Loved

HEY, LOVE,

We've met before somewhere. We've bumped into each other in the bathroom at a conference or a restaurant, refreshing our makeup, maybe changing a baby's diaper. We've seen each other in fitting rooms, standing in front of a mirror under intimidating lighting. *Is this outfit me?* we ask ourselves, instinctively holding in our stomachs.

We've lived in front of mirrors all our lives—in school bathrooms, clothing-store fitting rooms, locker rooms, and our bedrooms. And they've been our harshest critics.

For me, the mirror is not only where I come face to face with my body (as if that were not enough). It's where I'm forced to face myself. My personality, who I've been, what I've done, who I fully am. I stand before the mirror and ask, "Am I okay?"

I've learned, and continue to learn, that it's easy to grant power and authority to these inanimate objects we know as mirrors. I'll never get a satisfactory answer from this reflecting object attached to a wall. The mirror is an echo chamber that bounces back my own thoughts about me. There's more to me than how certain clothing fits; there's more to me than my changing body. There always has been.

It's not possible for a mirror to know your worth. It can't make an assessment of your beauty or how smart and kind you are. It cannot tell you about your potential.

To explore all that, you have to go much deeper. And that can be even harder, because you have to make all the parts of yourself so vulnerable.

What would it be like to be seen fully and known intimately and still be loved unconditionally? I mean beyond your body to the you on the inside. What if you were known and loved entirely? Every part of your story, every fragile weakness, every quirk, every talent, everything. Nothing hidden, nothing overlooked, and still you are surrounded and enfolded by love.

How might that change you? What would you see then, when you looked in the mirror?

xo,

Jo

⁓

You'd be so pretty if you weren't so dark skinned."
"Stay out of the sun so you won't get even darker."
"Your lips are so big."
"Your nose is too broad."

"You should go on a diet."

"Men don't like tall women."

"You're exotic!"

"I like you and I'm attracted to you, but I can't date you because you're black."

I stood silently in front of a mirror with the thoughts and opinions of others echoing through my head. Some were passing comments from acquaintances, some were the voices of opinionated strangers who felt compelled to share unsolicited advice. Some were the spoken thoughts of the guys I hung out with.

The Bible reminds us that the words we use have power (see Proverbs 18:21; James 3). And words that assess our looks, our intelligence, our potential, our personalities, our desirability—those are the words that have the power to destroy. It didn't matter that I didn't agree with the unfair and inaccurate comments. The words still hit me like damning accusations.

I was being judged before I was even known. I was seventeen or eighteen years old and locked in a battle over my body that I was tired of losing.

The battle, which often felt more like an attack because it was that one sided, was fought on multiple fronts. When I looked in fashion magazines or watched television shows and movies, I rarely saw anyone who looked like me. The women celebrated as beautiful never looked like me. Back then I didn't know about airbrushing or Photoshop. I didn't know that the women I saw in magazines didn't look like that in real life. As the stunning supermodel Cindy Crawford is famous for saying, "Even I don't wake up looking like Cindy Crawford."

In addition, it was rare to see a woman with my skin tone. I'm forever grateful for the fleeting images of models such as Iman and Naomi Campbell, women such as Oprah Winfrey and Phylicia Rashad. Seeing these smart, talented, dynamic women making a difference in the world had a profound impact. Still, they were greatly outnumbered by white women. The overwhelming majority of media images that I saw seemed to suggest that I was too dark skinned and too big to have value. As I flipped through a magazine or watched television, all I saw and heard were messages that I was somehow wrong. Not my views, beliefs, or commitments in life. But me, the physical person, the young black woman.

And then there was the damage done by what I *didn't* see and hear. The absence of someone like me sent a message to my heart. I did not belong with the beautiful, the popular, or the worthy. I was virtually invisible.

Alongside this barrage of criticism, my body grew awkwardly and erratically throughout my teen years. It wasn't all bad. My singing voice grew loud and strong. I finally liked its tone again. I was a great athlete and enjoyed discovering what my body could do on the playing field. Discovering my speed and strength was a faint signpost of grace in an otherwise confusing time of my life.

Nonetheless, the sudden growth wasn't all good. My feet grew relentlessly, as did my arms and legs. I was never great at putting an outfit together, so I was always the last to notice my ill-fitting clothes. I couldn't afford the new clothes I would need to keep up with the cool girls anyway. So I spent my days feeling uncomfortable inside and out. My efforts were never good enough, so I was never good enough.

When I stepped into my home, I stepped into a Nigerian world that upheld different standards of beauty. At home, my black skin was affirmed; it always had been. We didn't talk about our bodies much; why would we? At home I wasn't *different*; I wasn't *other*; I was just normal—a tall black girl. Furthermore, we were expected to work toward goals that had far more value than superficial appearances.

Who has time to talk about the current definition of *pretty* and the subjective value placed on being thin when you're an immigrant trying to build a new life and a future in England? *My dear, focus on what matters,* I can hear the voices of my aunties telling me. Our priority was to get a good education to prepare us for a strong career. Looking back, I wonder if not talking through my struggles with body image left a vacuum into which popular culture whispered lies and the Enemy of our souls deposited his poison. My lack of self-assurance combined with the lies of popular culture and attacks from the Enemy produced a toxic cocktail that was as corrosive as acid.

When I faced a mirror, I stood there clothed in awkward adolescent vulnerability, accessorized with bouts of self-loathing, layered with years of conflicting opinions regarding my worth. Like most of us, I discounted the affirmations of my beauty, intelligence, strength, and value. Rather, I sided with opinions that devalued who I was. All I could hear was negativity and judgment.

My looks were not enough; my body was not enough. It didn't matter if the critics didn't know me, the verdict was already in: I was not acceptable.

## What Story Does Your Mirror Tell You?

Have you ever stood in front of one of those distorting mirrors at a carnival or a state fair? You know the glass is oddly shaped but you don't know what you'll see when you look into it. Your eyes are huge, your legs are tiny, and your arms are completely twisted! It's a bit of a shock, the distortion.

Still, it's possible you live each day surrounded by distorted mirrors, and it's no funhouse experience. This time it's not the tricks of concave and convex segments of curved mirrors. This time the distortions come from a source much closer, and as such it is much more potent. The distortions come from what you think about yourself.

You're too tall; you're too small; you're too thin; your hips are too wide. Without warning the critique goes deeper. Your voice is too loud; you are too strong and direct. Or you're too emotional, too sensitive, too weak, flighty. It's there in the mirror for all to see, and all you can do is look away and try not to think about it.

Kelsey was happy with her shape, but continually had to fend off the diet suggestions and weird, passive-aggressive "should you be eating that?" comments from her siblings. When her sister announced her engagement, Kelsey was excited but felt a hint of dread when she was asked to be a bridesmaid. She knew her body would be under scrutiny in the coming months. What kind of expectations would her sister have?

It's strange that even when we reject the distorted views of our culture, we still feel the weight of their burden and shame. Maureen refreshed her makeup in the bathroom before the team meeting with a new client. She enjoyed her role at work and felt secure about being one of the older members of her team. (Some of her colleagues were the same age as her children.) But one thing unsettled her. Any time she received a compliment, it was praise for looking younger than she was. These compliments often were expressed with surprise. It wasn't just the implication that older was somehow negative. Maureen had raised children, rebuilt her life after divorce, and retrained professionally. She brought in new clients, building the business. None of this was negative, and who else on the team was as accomplished? But all they could say was that she looked younger than her age?

Susan Barry, retired neuroscientist and professor, has described our body image as "integral to our sense of identity," noting that it changes and gets updated in accordance with the information we receive.[1] So what information are we receiving? All too often the mirror tells you a distorted story with pieces contributed by multiple sources. It's almost inevitable that you succumb to the distortions from time to time, believing that the dream version of you is found in possessing the dream body. Yet the truth is that even a real mirror—one without visual distortion—can offer nothing more than an incomplete story. It can capture what you look like on any given day. It might reveal a glimpse of how you feel as re-vealed in your facial expression and body language. But it can't tell who you are or determine your value.

It's a mirror. It doesn't know you.

## SEEN, KNOWN, LOVED?

When God broke into my world and revealed that He was my heavenly Father, I encountered a love that saw me and knew me. But I wasn't entirely sure how to relate to God. I knew Jesus had died for me. I knew how to pray, and I saw prayers answered. I read the Bible and studied in groups. I worshipped; I prayed to be filled with the Holy Spirit. My faith was sincere and earnest. But I still didn't know how to feel important to God, to feel secure in His love. Was a Father's love big enough to overcome the doubts and accusations that faced me in the mirror? Could His words speak something new and life-giving that would update my understanding of my body image and so my identity? I didn't know how to make God's anchoring love a daily reality.

"It's God's responsibility to get it through to you," the pastor told me on that tissue-drenched, mascara-smudged night at church. And piece by piece, God did get the truth of His love through to me. One of the most compelling ways was through the Bible, particularly through some Old Testament figures I read about. I was drawn to their stories, the texture of their covenant relationship with God in action in the midst of their earthy humanity. I needed the examples of people whose lives were not neatly sewn together. I needed to see God's love transforming the arc of a person's life.

One character stood out for me above all the others: David.

## GOD KNEW THE BEST AND WORST OF DAVID—AND LOVED HIM

We first meet David as a teenaged shepherd, the youngest son in his family. When Samuel, the nation's judge, visited David's family, no one even considered bringing David in from the fields to meet this important guest. (How would you like it if your dad failed to let you know the Queen of England was in the living room paying a call?) It was only when Samuel specifically asked Jesse, David's father, if he had any more sons that we learn that David even existed.

Perhaps it was good that David remained unacknowledged by his immediate family. As we read his story, we find that David's family system did not define him, nor did it limit him. David was the youngest son, assigned to watch sheep, and he became a warrior, a military leader, and Israel's greatest king.

Yet while David ruled Israel during the nation's golden era, he remained a tremendous leader with outsized flaws. He was so relentlessly bullied by his predecessor, King Saul, that it cost him everything. He was a man who lost a rare, irreplaceable friend (see 2 Samuel 1:25–26). He committed adultery and, in a cowardly attempt to cover up his lust, conspired to have a faithful man murdered (see 2 Samuel 11). He made glaring mistakes concerning his children (see 2 Samuel 13). He knew great suffering and great fame (see 1 Samuel 18–19). He wanted to build a Temple for God but was not allowed to because his military campaigns meant he had too much blood on his hands (see 1 Chronicles 22:7–8).

Complex as he was, David also was given the incredible accolade that he was a man after God's own heart (see 1 Samuel 13:14). In the Bible's books of history, you find the narrative of David's journey. But it's in Psalms, the Bible's book of songs, poetry, and prayers, that you read the story of his soul. A prolific songwriter and worshipper, David is the attributed author of seventy-five psalms. They are songs drawn from his shepherd days (see Psalm 23), from his years as a fugitive in the wilderness (see Psalm 63; 64), and from his time as Israel's leader (see Psalm 122). There are confessions made after he committed adultery and had Uriah killed (see Psalm 51) and pleas for God's mercy as David's son Absalom sought to steal the throne (see Psalm 3–5). There are songs of sorrow and lament, declarations of praise and wonder.

David crafted songs of rich theological insight and incredible faith that continue to speak to and connect with the human condition. One psalm in particular began to speak to my condition, revealing that I was fully known and deeply loved, grounding my identity and redeeming every part of my story.

## Psalm 139

For the director of music. Of David. A psalm.

[1]O Lord, you have searched me
    and you know me.
[2]You know when I sit and when I rise;
    you perceive my thoughts from afar.
[3]You discern my going out and my lying down;
    you are familiar with all my ways.
[4]Before a word is on my tongue
    you know it completely, O Lord.

[5]You hem me in—behind and before;
    you have laid your hand upon me.
[6]Such knowledge is too wonderful for me,
    too lofty for me to attain.

[7]Where can I go from your Spirit?
    Where can I flee from your presence?
[8]If I go up to the heavens, you are there;
    if I make my bed in the depths, you are there.
[9]If I rise on the wings of the dawn,
    if I settle on the far side of the sea,
[10]even there your hand will guide me,
    your right hand will hold me fast.

[11]If I say, "Surely the darkness will hide me
    and the light become night around me,"
[12]even the darkness will not be dark to you;
    the night will shine like the day,
    for darkness is as light to you.

<sup>13</sup>For you created my inmost being;

    you knit me together in my mother's womb.

<sup>14</sup>I praise you because I am fearfully and wonderfully made;

    your works are wonderful,

    I know that full well.

<sup>15</sup>My frame was not hidden from you

    when I was made in the secret place.

When I was woven together in the depths of the earth,

    <sup>16</sup>your eyes saw my unformed body.

All the days ordained for me

    were written in your book

    before one of them came to be.


<sup>17</sup>How precious to me are your thoughts, O God!

    How vast is the sum of them!

<sup>18</sup>Were I to count them,

    they would outnumber the grains of sand.

When I awake,

    I am still with you.


<sup>19</sup>If only you would slay the wicked, O God!

    Away from me, you bloodthirsty men!

<sup>20</sup>They speak of you with evil intent;

    your adversaries misuse your name.

<sup>21</sup>Do I not hate those who hate you, O LORD,

    and abhor those who rise up against you?

<sup>22</sup>I have nothing but hatred for them;

    I count them my enemies.

[23]Search me, O God, and know my heart;

    test me and know my anxious thoughts.

[24]See if there is any offensive way in me,

    and lead me in the way everlasting. (NIV)

I love that a complex man, with a full and complex life, wrote this psalm. It's tempting to treat this psalm in a romantic or sentimental way, imagining a gentle musical soundtrack and delicate watercolor scenes. Something that is suitable for a book like *Moments of Serenity* or an inspirational calendar. (Except, that is, for verses 19 through 22, which initially are so discordant it's tempting to just overlook them.)

Yet the rhapsodies were coming out of David's raw, gritty, sometimes dangerous life. According to Rabbi Ibn Ezra, Psalm 139 was the crown of all of David's psalms.[2] It communicates God's majesty alongside an awareness of God's presence and involvement in the intimate parts of life. The psalm speaks of what it means to be fully seen and known. For David, that meant being seen and known as both worshipper and warrior, shepherd and giant-slayer, fugitive and father, even as adulterer and killer. And yes, as king.

The opening notes of Psalm 139 remind us that David's personal song is meant to be used in public worship. It's a psalm for everyone, a psalm written in the key of life both then and now. And most important to you and me, he wrote this psalm for all of us. Who has not been so desperate, due to circumstances of life, that she has cried out in pain and the fading hope that there might still be help available? This psalm played a decisive role as God began to reveal my identity and redeem my story. It began by addressing the most physical evidence of my identity.

## TELLING OURSELVES THE TRUTH TO SILENCE THE LIES

> For you created my inmost being;
>> you knit me together in my mother's womb.
> I praise you because I am fearfully and wonder-
>> fully made;
>> your works are wonderful,
>> I know that full well. (Psalm 139:13–14, NIV)

When you read the Bible, do you ever find that certain words jump out like flashing lights? And while you try to keep reading, do you find that your mind, your eyes, and just perhaps a slice of your soul keep calling you back to the flashing verses? This is what happened during a devotional time when I arrived at Psalm 139 and when I read these verses in particular.

The verses confronted my identity, revealing where I had exchanged God's truth for lies. I had handed over the beauty of who I was—who God said very clearly I was—for lots of painful, damaging lies.

"I praise you because I am fearfully and wonderfully made."

At the time, I couldn't read those words and mean them. The truth they held seemed to be the opposite of what I felt. Yet I knew God wanted me to see His view on creating me. He wanted me to see the lies for what they were, lies that chained me, that poisoned me. I knew He wanted me to exchange the voices of the culture, the lies, and my own insecurity—everything that named my body as useless—for His truth. I'd bought into the lies, felt the weight of shame for so long. It was time to invest in some truth.

I took my Bible and stood in front of the mirror. I felt prompted to read my neon-light verse over every single part of my body, out loud. Especially over the parts I didn't like or felt I should be ashamed of. I began, starting with the parts of me that I liked!

"I thank You, Lord, that my eyes are fearfully and wonderfully made . . . for my teeth . . .

"I praise You, Lord, that my ebony skin is fearfully and wonderfully made. Your works are wonderful; I know that full well. I am not too dark for You. This is me. And it's good. I'm good? Yes, I'm good!

"I praise You, Lord, for my ears. Personally, I think they're too small, but You say they are fearfully and wonderfully made. Fine.

"I thank You for my stomach. I promise to stop calling it my nemesis, to stop saying that I hate it. But this is so hard. Why can't it be flat? And why do I have stretch marks? I'm a teenager!

"I know I'm supposed to thank You for my feet, but right now I need You to stop them from growing because my favorite shoe store is running out of options for my size. Please God.

"Your works are wonderful. And I guess that includes me."

With that, the fierce battle over my body intensified. What was the truth: what I felt and heard and interpreted in the culture, or what God spoke over me through a psalm? Which would be the louder voice in my life? That's when I discovered that the Bible is a weapon, the sword of the Spirit (see Ephesians 6:17). It was when I stood in front of that mirror and read Psalm 139 that I first felt the weight of the sword in my hand and began to discover its impact as an offensive weapon. I read the psalm daily, sometimes multiple times through the day, thanking God that I was fearfully and wonderfully made.

I'd read the psalm as I looked into the mirror, then I'd write it down. Sometimes I prayed, trembling through my tears, arguing with God about the body parts I found the hardest to accept, then sobbing my way into surrender. Other times I felt victorious. These words affirmed my beautiful black skin! God created my skin tone. I was right; my skin tone *is* beautiful, just like every skin tone He created. I am going to stand in the sun, and I'm going to wear good-quality sunscreen because of the lack of an ozone layer. And I'm going to get darker like I always do, and I'm going to love my glow because I'm made in His image and that's a good thing.

Yet honestly, I'd reread Psalm 139 many times and feel nothing. It was just hard work, repetitive, dull at times, made up of blood, sweat, and tears. It was a personal war as well as a path to transformation. Speaking God's Word over every part of my body started as a discipline until it became a habit, until it became my rhythm, until it became my life. I learned that just because I wasn't feeling changed didn't mean I wasn't *being* changed.

I didn't realize that every time I declared that verse, I was cutting away at chains, slicing and splicing the most seductive and stealthy of lies. I didn't know that God's words had fallen like seed in the soil of my heart, growing in the dark, taking root until they broke my life open into a new dawn.

## WHAT IS REFLECTED IN YOUR MIRROR?

What do you see when you look in the mirror?

I think of the journeys taken by women I know and women I've met, the storms they weathered and how they had to fight to establish themselves. I think of the women who were victims of abuse, violence, and violation, courageous survivors who want to become whole.

The women who live on the other side of eating disorders. On most days, they walk free and far from the past. And then there are other days.

Some women stand in front of a mirror and grieve because, though a medical treatment saved their lives, it also cost them their hair, their nails, their brows for a time. Or their breasts, permanently.

There are the women who lay a hand near their womb and question their worth because they never carried a child. Others who lay their hand on that same space ache that their bodies could not carry a much-loved precious new life to term.

> You are fully known. He has seen it all and He knows it all. And still you are deeply, deeply loved.

There are others who see a person they used to be. In their closets are the sizes they used to wear. They feel the shame of still caring about the difference.

Some of you haven't stood in front of a full-length mirror for quite some time now. You step to the edges when family photos are being taken, or you only take pictures of the children. It's simply too hard to see yourself in photos.

Some of you take pictures, but they're never candid. They are staged, filtered, positioned until they are Instagram-worthy. You don't mean to count the "Likes," note the comments. You tell yourself you don't want to care. But every click on social media has become a statement about your body and your value. You don't want it to matter so much to you. But it does.

You are fully known. He has seen it all and He knows it all. And still you are deeply, deeply loved.

> Search me, O God, and know my heart;
>      test me and know my anxious thoughts.
> Point out anything in me that offends you,
>      and lead me along the path of everlasting life.
>           (Psalm 139:23–24)

Even though these verses come at the end of the psalm, I often use these words as an opening prayer. Sometimes it's my way of inviting God to argue my case against my inner voices. Sometimes it's a way for me to slow down to see where I am. In relation to my body and who I am, these words scan my heart, my mind, my everything. They've led me back to my flashing-light verses. They've leveled me and liberated me.

I am not who anyone but God says I am. I am not even who *I* say I am, or more often, who I fear I might be. I am God's, and only God can identify me truly.

Perhaps the words of Psalm 139:23–24 can be your first words as you stand in front of the mirror. Invite God to meet you right then, in that moment, before any other voice can intrude. Then wait. And then begin. Using Psalm 139:14, acknowledge that your body, your personality, your talents, all of you is fearfully and wonderfully made.

There will be other verses, psalms, chapters, and books from the Bible that God highlights for you. The words will shout at you and won't allow you to keep reading until you take the brightly lit words to heart. The dark recesses of your struggling will fall to God's offensive weapon—the sword of the Spirit, the truth, the only words you can always, without reservation, trust.

Take hold of them, write them down, put them on your phone, and write them on your mirror if you need to. His words have the power to level and liberate you, a Spirit-filled sword to cut through the most resistant of chains. I think they can help you see into the mirror differently.

His words help you discover who you fully are. His words speak a truth that will set you free.

# 7

# Slay Your Giants

HEY THERE, GIANT-KILLER,

I know that title is the opposite of how you feel, but it's a worthy name to describe you and the moment you're in. You are moving forward, reclaiming your identity and acknowledging your voice. You experience moments of hope and freedom; you catch glimpses of your potential and promise. And at the moment it feels good.

But it's also a long, hard battle. You knew it wasn't going to be easy. You are choosing to uproot entrenched patterns of thinking and ways of being. You're refusing to live by the powerful lies about God, as well as the lies about you and your body and your place in the world. You are daring to live differently in the face of feelings and habits that have held you back for years.

It's understandable that as you do this you feel you're at your smallest. It's intimidating. It makes you wish you felt braver, stronger somehow. Feeling so weak disappoints you.

Sister, you may not feel brave or strong, but the fact that you are engaging with some of the deepest parts of you, that you're attending to the broken fragments of your life, points to the truth of your strength and tenacity.

Also, *never forget that you are not alone. You have a covenant Partner who sees you and fights for you. It's not who you are that makes you a giant-killer, it's whose you are. Now you are a force to be reckoned with. He will help you face everything that tries to block your path. Today your fears might seem to tower over you, but in time you will see that in Him you tower over fears that dared to stand in your way.*

*Go slay,*

Jo

෴

One of my favorite pastimes is reading with my daughters. As toddlers, they were enamored of pictures in books and stories that included songs. Now that they are older, their book choices serve to help them discover their interests and passions. Reading is a springboard for processing together, as they learn to navigate their way through the world. Sometimes when we read together, I end up getting into the book more than they do!

One such book is *Courage for Beginners* by Karen Harrington. The author tells the story of Mysti Murphy, a seventh grader whose life unravels when her father, the strength and cement of her family, is injured in an accident. He is forced to spend months in the hospital. Mysti's father's condition forces her to confront the family secret: her mother never leaves the house.

Meanwhile, Mysti's best friend turns on her and begins bullying her at school. Mysti must deal with her looming struggles to survive the school year.

She takes brave steps to move forward by learning to shop for groceries and cook for the family. She finds new friends. She performs in the school talent show despite the bully's cruelty. She even challenges her mom to name her agoraphobia and acknowledge its impact on the family. Mysti's journey is vulnerable, overwhelming at times. But by the end of the school year she finds the strength to be herself—she finds her voice and starts using it. Courage for beginners, indeed.[1]

Mysti's growing pains resonate deeply with me. It has been a vulnerable struggle for me to let go of the past and live into my purpose. Like Mysti, I've faced towering challenges and overwhelming obstacles. I've never felt strong or courageous enough. Yet facing gigantic challenges was the beginning of freedom. It forced me to shed old ways of thinking and being, and it opened up a way to the life I was created for.

It seems that when God redeems a person's identity and leads her to her purpose, there's a backdrop of battle and vulnerability. We saw it in Esther's journey when she had to address the king to save her people. If you're going to embrace your God-given identity, reclaim your voice, and live out your purpose, it will be a fight. You'll need to learn how to name, confront, and slay the giants that stand in the way of the life you were made for.

David's first battle in front of spectators serves as a great example to teach us how to slay our giants.

## From Overlooked Shepherd
## to Giant Slayer

When Israel had to face an old and brutal enemy, the army began to discover who David was. Until this point he had been an overlooked teenaged shepherd and later, a harpist for King Saul. His service in the king's court suggested there was more to David than his harp (see 1 Samuel 16:18). But he didn't find his voice until he volunteered to attempt what no other warrior in Israel's army dared to do.

The Philistine army had camped between Socoh and Azekah at Ephes-dammim, which is understood to be on the south side of today's Elah Valley in Israel. King Saul responded by positioning Israelite troops on the northern side. The two armies faced each other from the crests of not-too-distant hills, with nothing to stop a clash of forces but the valley between. Saul had been a successful military leader in the earlier years of his reign. But by this point, the breakdown of his relationship with the Lord was increasingly evident, first privately in the royal court where he needed soothing from torment and fear and soon out in public as the Philistines taunted Israel to come out and fight.

During the stalemate of inactivity, the Gentile army presented its secret weapon: Goliath of Gath. Goliath was the Philistine champion warrior for good reason. He stood between eight and nine feet tall and wore bronze armor weighing about one hundred twenty-six pounds. The tip of his javelin alone weighed fifteen pounds. His presence inspired confidence in every Philistine soldier and instilled terror in every Israelite who saw him. Saul was not immune from the fear.

Goliath taunted the Israelites, calling them to present their best fighter for one-on-one combat. The winner would determine the outcome of the war and the future of the people. Whoever lost would be slaves of the winner.

As king of Israel and leader of the army, Saul should have gone out to face the giant. Goliath knew it; all the Philistines knew it. The Israelites knew it. Saul knew it too, but he refused to perform his duty. Goliath repeated his challenge for forty days and nights, mocking Israel's army with every word.

Then David the shepherd boy arrived on the scene. After hearing Goliath's insults and watching the timid reaction of his people, David offered to take down the giant once and for all.

## FACING YOUR GIANTS

There was only one Goliath of Gath, but David had to slay several giants before he even arrived at the battlefield. His other enemies weren't visible; they were the gigantic internal challenges that threatened to destroy his mind and heart. You and I have never faced a physical giant in full battle array. But as we embrace our identity and purpose, we will face gigantic challenges that turn the landscape of our hearts and minds into a battleground.

David's journey to the battlefield points out some of the giants we'll face, and it shows how to defeat them. Prepare to slay your giants.

## Giant Number 1

First in line is the giant that makes you feel small and intends to keep you feeling that way. David's father, Jesse, sent him to the camp of Israel's army to deliver supplies to his brothers. David was to give them the items their father had sent, then return to Jesse with news of his sons' well-being (see 1 Samuel 17:17–19). Jesse had a limited view of David's potential.

Remember when Samuel the prophet arrived at Jesse's home in search of God's choice for King Saul's successor? David was overlooked, left with the sheep out in the fields. In Jesse's mind, there was no way his youngest son could be God's pick for a future king. David? No, he was just a boy.

The pattern continued when Jesse sent David to deliver supplies, failing to acknowledge that David's reputation as a warrior already had been established in Saul's court (see 1 Samuel 16:18). Perhaps Jesse had other reasons for wanting to discount David's potential. He was an old man with three sons at the battle line. Maybe Jesse simply was not ready to release yet another son to the dangers of war. Whatever his reasoning, Jesse's attitude toward David potentially stood in the way of David's fulfilling his calling and purpose.

David delivered the supplies and checked on his brothers. At this point he could return home to report to his father. But after hearing Goliath's taunts and seeing the Israelite army cower in fear (see 1 Samuel 17:24), David spoke up.

"What will a man get for killing this Philistine and ending his defiance of Israel? Who is this pagan Philistine anyway, that he is allowed to defy the armies of the living God?" (1 Samuel 17:26).

David clearly did not buy the party line that Goliath was invincible. (We'll return to that later.) With two daring questions, David stepped away from behaving like a dutiful son. If David had settled for being an overlooked shepherd and delivery boy, he would have silenced his voice and forfeited his calling. He would not have changed the course of history. Instead of obeying his father, he spoke and acted like a brave warrior. The shepherd boy was walking into his calling.

You might be thinking, *Well, sure, this was God's anointed, the greatest king of Israel. But what about me?* Each of us has a calling, and each of us runs into forces that try to limit us and silence our voice. Sometimes the giant appears in the expectations others have placed on us. Like Jesse with David, people see what they need us to be; they don't see all that we already are. Sometimes we can't step into all that God has for us because of the duties and expectations we place on ourselves. We run errands when God has designed us to slay giants. We settle for a smaller, safer life.

We're held back by the giant's insults: "Who do you think you are? You're just a mom; you're just a woman; you're too young; you're too old. Listen, just leave the dreaming to the big boys." Or in the name of limiting us, the giant begs us to hold on to the safety of our insecurities and be content with the status quo.

Looking back, it seems I was the last to realize that I'd already been using my voice and finding my purpose through leadership. The teachers at my school knew this, because I often was asked to captain a sports team or take a leadership role in class. They knew at church. When I attended a Christian youth event, I felt compelled to do anything or go anywhere for God. I expected to be called to missions, and instead I was called to speak and lead. There was only one problem: I didn't want to be seen. I hid in the shadows. But when I told my church youth group leaders about what I felt God was asking of me, they began to train me and give me opportunities to speak. I shared my testimony, read prayers and liturgy, talked with a group of seniors in the church. For months I was literally sick with nerves every time I was due to speak. It was awful.

Years later I realized I needed to embrace my leadership calling. I'd find myself gazing across the valley, hearing the sneering taunts that repeated, "Who do you think you are? You belong in the shadows."

Would I settle for a life that kept me small, or would I allow myself to dream and explore what God could do if I put my life in His hands? I had to slay the giant.

> What could it look like to think, question, and act in the light of who God says you are, rather than the duties and expectations that have bound you?

If you want to slay your own giant, consider David's story. First, carry out the errand you were given, but don't leave the scene just yet. Look at the world in front of you, remember the dreams and ideas that refuse to leave your mind and soul. Instead of staying confined, get curious about God's dream for your purpose in life.

To slay my giant, I had to stop listening to the "Who do you think you are?" line and replace it with a question about what I saw happening. *God, these leadership opportunities won't go away. And the speaking opportunities terrify me. But I must ask You: What do You want me to do? What is Your dream for my life?*

What could it look like to think, question, and act in the light of who God says you are, rather than the duties and expectations that have bound you?

### Giant Number 2

Some giants are not just one obstacle or one force, but an ill-defined yet noisy lot known as "they." Too many of us choose not to use our voices because we are worried about what "they"—either real people or perceived judgment of us—will think.

"When David's oldest brother, Eliab, heard David talking to the [soldiers], he was angry. 'What are you doing around here anyway?' he demanded. 'What about those few sheep you're supposed to be taking care of? I know about your pride and deceit'" (1 Samuel 17:28).

The New International Version of the Bible states that Eliab "burned with anger" when he heard David speaking with the soldiers of Israel. Why? Was he embarrassed by David's out-loud wonder that none of God's soldiers would stand up to Goliath? Was he jealous of David? Perhaps Eliab hadn't forgotten that David received the recognition and anointing from Samuel that everybody thought should have been Eliab's (see 1 Samuel 16:6–7, 11–13).

Eliab's anger turned to derision. He questioned David's presence in the army camp, suggesting he had no place there. He belittled David's shepherding, and finally, he attacked David's character, accusing him of arrogance and deceit.

David responded, "What have I done now? . . . I was only asking a question!" (1 Samuel 17:29). David fell back on the classic youngest-sibling response, proclaiming his innocence. And instead of being knocked off course by the wounding accusations, David simply ignored his brother and talked to other soldiers. He would not turn back because of what his brother—a giant of shame and derision—had said to him.

Monica found a giant of shame and derision in a most unexpected place. It had been months since Monica had seen Christie, her former mentor. They met in their favorite coffee shop, the one where they'd met during Monica's time in grad school. Christie had been influential in Monica's life and continued to be a reference point for wisdom at significant stages in her career. Monica was bursting to tell Christie that she had been invited to apply for an exciting new position at work. She'd be able to build a new team and undertake some dynamic projects.

When Monica shared her excitement, Christie asked, "Don't you think you're being a bit ambitious? You don't have the experience for this job. I bet they've asked lots of people to apply, but they already know who they want," implying it couldn't be Monica. Christie leaned forward. "Let's face it, Monica. You brought some diversity to the résumé pile, that's all. Don't even apply. It'll be humiliating."

Blindsided by Christie's comments, Monica didn't know where to turn. She smiled weakly, removed Christie's hand from her arm, and sipped her coffee. The topic changed, and Monica tried to stay engaged in conversation, nodding and murmuring in all the right places. But she felt utterly embarrassed. She checked the time, waiting long enough before she said she needed to leave.

Imagine the voices of giants of derision you might hear on a fairly regular basis:

You want to organize a neighborhood gathering? Do you realize you haven't lived here as long as most of the women on the street?

Start a business? Well, I hope you've done your research. Do you realize the economy is slowing down and women entrepreneurs often find it tough to get a business loan? It's natural and healthy to be aware of what people think of you. But when the approval of others determines if and how you live into your purpose, you're facing (and giving into) a big giant.

Sometimes we hear discrediting messages that really take the wind out of our sails because they come from people who are close to us. People we expected to champion us do just the opposite and belittle us.

On other occasions the giant called "they" isn't about what people have said or done; it's about what they *might* say or what they *might* think. The fear of rejection is so strong that it's easier for us to just hold back. Yet when we step back due to what someone might say, we avoid God's invitation to join Him in what He is doing in the world.

After serving as a volunteer at my church throughout college, I was offered a staff position. I was young and naive; I got a lot of things wrong (still do!) and learned a lot (still do that too!). In the years that followed, I was offered opportunities to serve beyond my local church, speaking at conferences around the country and the world. It was an intimidating privilege. My local church was my home and my spiritual family. We knew each other; it was safe. But traveling to minister in other areas was uncharted territory. What would they think of me?

Even as part of the staff at my local church, I often was the youngest person in a meeting. What did they think of my perspective? Many times I was the only woman at the table. Did they really want me there? I was almost always the only woman of color present. Did they see my contribution, or did they think I was there as a token gesture toward diversity?

And if I was traveling to speak, some of the same questions nearly paralyzed me. All the second-guessing made me nervous and wore me out, exactly as my giant enemy intended.

David initially pushed back at his brother Eliab, but rather than defend himself forever and be worn out by the verbal battle, ultimately he ignored Eliab and kept pursuing his calling. In whatever form you are confronted by the giant known as "they," you have to slay it. Often the battle strategy is, much like David's, to simply walk away from the conversation. (This includes the conversations in your mind.) Instead, you walk toward what God is already doing. It's not easy, but fighting for their approval is not your calling. Walking into what God is doing is your calling.

Stop and consider:

- As you pursue your purpose, what are you afraid "they" will say or do?
- In which practical ways can you move beyond the words of accusers into where God is leading you?

### Giant Number 3

David had volunteered for service, even though he was not at that time a member of the army. "What will a man get for killing this Philistine and ending his defiance of Israel?" the shepherd boy asked. "Who is this pagan Philistine anyway, that he is allowed to defy the armies of the living God?" (1 Samuel 17:26).

Eventually David's inquiry reached King Saul's ears, and David was summoned. David told the king he would deal with Israel's giant problem. The God who helped him protect his father's sheep from predators would also help him deal with this Philistine predator (see 1 Samuel 17:37–38). Saul tried to get David to wear his kingly armor, but it was far too large. David declined and instead selected five stones to use in his sling. David had the armor of his story with God, forged in his many battle experiences protecting sheep.

Still, the teenager was at a distinct physical mismatch going against Goliath. I'm stunned by David's courage. With the armies of Israel and Philistia watching what the soldiers must have assumed would be a slaughter, David called out the giant—secure in what he had with God. God was enough.

This third giant traps us into comparison. We feel that what we bring isn't good enough; we dismiss our ideas and values and skills, believing someone else's approach is better. Sometimes we'll even try their lifestyle on for size, even though it doesn't fit, because it looks so much better than ours. How many times have I compared myself with other people and felt inadequate? I have thought, *If I had their shiny story, if I had their shiny strong connections, if I had what they have, I could slay giants!*

But what I need is what I already have: God's story in my life and what He already has given me. If that looks like pebbles and a sling, then that is enough.

As you walk toward your purpose, it's easy to want to suit up in the king's armor so you'll feel ready. In fact, the giant you face will taunt you, saying you are ill-equipped and not enough. But it's a lie. Remember David.

You don't need to wear someone else's armor. Your story with God, your own gifts, will take down giants. Even if they look like nothing but pebbles.

How does comparison overshadow you and your identity and purpose? What could it look like to pick up and use the skills and gifts (the armor) God has given you?

### Giant Number 4

Even if the giant you face is Goliath, when God is your covenant Partner the giant is small. Goliath of Gath saw David and cursed him. David responded: "You come to me with sword, spear, and javelin, but I come to you in the name of the LORD of Heaven's Armies—the God of the armies of Israel, whom you have defied. Today the LORD will conquer you, and I will kill you" (1 Samuel 17:45–46).

David ran toward Goliath and killed the Philistine with a sling and a stone just as he said he would. Shocked and terrified, the Philistine soldiers ran for their lives. Now emboldened, the Israelites gave chase and overpowered the Philistines.

While everyone else feared the big, strong, powerful opponent, David was preoccupied with what Goliath *wasn't*. Twice David referred to the giant as a "pagan Philistine" (verses 26, 36). In the New International Version, David called the enemy an "uncircumcised Philistine." While it appears that David is insulting Goliath's manhood, he was rather making a deeply theological point. Israel's warriors were circumcised, a mark of their covenant with God (see Genesis 17). Their covenant Partner provided protection. When the Lord Almighty is your covenant Partner, giants are shown to be small.

David was confident in battle because he understood his relationship with God. David knew whose he was and who he was living for. He was overlooked and underestimated, but that didn't define him. Even his brother's accusations couldn't throw him off track. Because he knew whose he was and who he was, David wouldn't wear another person's armor, nor would he accept the story given to him by his father or his brother. David knew that it was God, his covenant Partner, who had conquered Goliath.

When we know whose we are, we can slay every giant that stands between us and our calling. You might be overlooked or belittled. You might be afraid of your dreams and your already proven potential. You might compare yourself to others and feel inadequate. But towering above all these giants is your covenant Partner, the Lord Almighty. He knows your name. He sees you and He loves you. And because of the sacrifice of His Son, He redeems your life and purpose. He slays your giants so you can move forward into all He has for you.

## Into the Wilderness

What happened after David felled the giant? Surely there must be a happily ever after? Not quite.

David's long journey had just begun. The years that followed were years of wonder interspersed with being hunted and having to hide out in the wilderness. David's wilderness experience was not unique. Many other biblical characters, such as Moses, Miriam, Joshua, Caleb, and Paul, experienced years of great wonder, but also endured a dry, extended exile in the wilderness. The way those characters navigated the changing terrain of their successes and struggles exposed fault lines in their souls and cracks in their identities.

The wilderness experience is a reality for us as well. It's where our foundations get tested and our weaknesses are revealed. It's where circumstances force us to question whose we are. The voices of opposition never stop accusing us because they don't want us to live in our God-given identities or speak with our God-given voices. They hunt us down, often when we're at our weakest. But that said, God is present with us in the wilderness because this stage is essential to our faith journey. We understand now that redemption and transformation are not one-off events; His redeeming love is still working on us and in us. Sometimes we must revisit old ground to keep moving forward into new life in Christ. So God meets us in the most unexpected places and in the most unexpected ways, even in the wilderness.

I just didn't expect the wilderness to meet me when we moved to America.

# 8

# The Wander Years

HEY, LOVE,

I see you wandering, looking and feeling like you lost your way.

You embraced your identity and voice with such hope and expectation. God offered you grace and you came running into love and life. You expected to go from strength to strength, pursuing a dynamic life with a secure identity and rich purpose. It was that way for a while, but it's nothing like that now.

It's hard to admit that there are days that have turned to weeks, months, and years where you feel quietly desperate. One of the hardest things to come to terms with is that the dream you are living is now the dream you prayed for.

It's just that the reality is not what you expected. It's not that you expected everything to be easy, but at the very minimum, in your dreams, God was close by. You could see His hand at work, always leading you forward as your faithful, strong covenant Partner. Now it seems that God caused the hard life you're living. Or perhaps it's that God somehow *is* the hard time.

Praying and reading the Bible feel empty and

pointless. It's as if God has stopped listening or—dare you think it—He has stopped caring.

Your dream didn't look anything like this. Your dream was full of color and beauty, possibility. This season is disappointing and frustrating. Maybe you should go back to living with your broken identity. At least you understood how to cope with it.

Sister, let me interpret this landscape for you. It is called the wilderness and it lives up to its name. It tests you to the core as you wonder how many breaking points you will reach. There's no end in sight.

But though it feels unbearably hard, I urge you not to walk away from all the progress you've made. I urge you not to look back. Because God is still here, working and moving—for you and in you—even through this difficult terrain. Stay engaged, stay the course.

Hang in there, Wander Woman,

Jo

༄

Finally, they were free.

Long after Joseph's work and legacy had been forgotten, the Israelites suffered greatly under the Egyptians and their pharaohs. Genocide, oppression, and slavery brutalized the Hebrew people. Desperate for justice and deliverance, they cried out for freedom. Remembering His covenant with Abraham, Isaac, Jacob, and Joseph, God called Moses out of Midian to represent Him before Pharaoh and to bring the Israelites out of Egypt.

Pharaoh ridiculed Moses's command to let the Israelites go. He even increased the slaves' suffering to try to turn them against Moses. Yet God used Moses to declare a series of plagues across Egypt that would humble Pharaoh. The final plague was the deaths of all of Egypt's firstborn boys. That carnage left no family untouched and finally brought Egypt to its knees. Pharaoh, after the death of his son, relented and released God's people.

A few hundred years after Joseph had given his sons names that recalled his own redemptive journey, the Israelites began their journey to deliverance and promise. The Bible records that six hundred thousand men, plus women and children, fled Egypt. Millions of people were suddenly free, taking flocks and herds of livestock with them (see Exodus 12:37–38). Imagine the noise, the confusion, the excitement, the heart-pounding departure from the land of their oppression. Men and women packed up their broken lives and walked, stumbled, ran into a new day. They left Rameses (modern-day Qantir) and began their life-changing adventure by desert road (see Exodus 3:18)

The Israelites were going to the Promised Land! It was described as a spacious land flowing with milk and honey (see Exodus 3:8; 13:5), symbolic of abundance, nurture, and life. They would have a home, their own home.

However, the journey to the land of promise was fraught with difficulty. First, the Egyptian army gave chase. After agreeing to let the people leave, Pharaoh changed his mind and tried to put a stop to their exodus (see Exodus 14). God intervened with a miraculous deliverance by creating a dry path through the Red Sea and, soon after, drowning Israel's enemies.

From the Red Sea, the Israelites went into the desert of Shur (thought to be Wadi Tumilat, east of the Nile delta). The wilderness journey was austere and difficult, marked by frustration as the people learned to survive in such a harsh environment. Mothers and fathers needed to feed their extended families, both the elderly and the young. The promise of milk and honey in the Promised Land must have sounded hollow when they couldn't even find water.

When the people grew desperate for food and water, they questioned God's presence and grumbled about their circumstances, lamenting that living in slavery was better than this (see Exodus 15:22–24; 16; 17:7). Seeds of disappointment and dissent were beginning to grow.

If all this were not enough, the wandering Israelites were attacked by the Amalekites. Even though God gave them victory, it was a reminder of their vulnerability. Who would attack them next? And if they *were* attacked again, where could they go? Were they vulnerable to every band of marauders that took a dislike to them? God had let them know that the Promised Land already was occupied. It wouldn't be easy to claim the land as their own.

Even amid their doubts and complaints, the wilderness was a significant place to encounter God. They enjoyed provisions of manna and quail and water from a rock. God's presence was near in the form of a pillar of cloud by day, and a pillar of fire by night. At Mount Sinai, the Israelites entered a covenant with God. They were given a new identity and purpose. Instead of slaves they were made "my kingdom of priests, my holy nation" treasured by God (Exodus 19:6). They were given guidance and instruction, and a framework within which to live out their new life and identity.

However, this covenant was soon forgotten. When Moses went up the mountain, the Israelites forgot their liberator and rejected God's covenant. Even Aaron the priest created a golden calf to worship, declaring a festival in its honor. The Israelites worshipped the way they had in the past, making sacrifices and offerings. Just as it was done in Egypt. Perhaps a golden calf felt more tangible than the cloud and fire off in the distance. The partying that went with calf worship certainly felt better than the survival mode they were living by. It wasn't milk and honey, but it was something.

## Defining the Wilderness

According to theologian David W. Baker, in the Hebrew Bible the wilderness referenced is more than the open desert of sand and palm trees. It was any geographical area that could not provide sufficient resources to sustain community life.[1] In addition, the wilderness bore spiritual significance.

It was a place of danger and vulnerability, but it was also a place of covenant and encountering God in power. It was a place of transition, the place between slavery and the Promised Land.[2] It also was the place of testing and transformation as the hearts of God's people were fully revealed.

So the wilderness became a place of deepening relationship or deep rebellion. These powerful wilderness experiences were not limited to the Exodus era or even just to the Old Testament.

In the wilderness, Hagar encountered God and named him El-roi, the "God who sees me."

David, the shepherd boy/giant-killer who would eventually become king, spent years in the wilderness hiding as a fugitive, in fear for his life.

The prophet Elijah hid and despaired in the wilderness when escaping Jezebel's death threats.

In the New Testament, John the Baptist conducted his entire ministry from the wilderness.

After John baptized Him, Jesus was driven by the Holy Spirit into the wilderness. There He fasted and prayed and faced the tempter.

God was always present with His beloved people in the wilderness. It is a profoundly spiritual place. But even with abundant examples in Scripture, when the wilderness experience makes up part of our faith journey, we may not always understand when and why it's happening.

## INTO THE WILDERNESS

My husband and I landed in the United States on June 22, 2004. We were wide-eyed newlyweds and ready for adventure. We spent two days in New York, shopping and walking around, just being tourists. We covered the highlights of Manhattan: the Guggenheim, Tribeca, Times Square, the Empire State Building. It was two days filled with fun and new experiences.

Then we boarded a flight to our new home in Phoenix, Arizona. I felt like I was on the verge of my destiny. When I had first visited the United States at age fourteen, something in me knew this was where I'd live one day. I'd tried to make it happen my own way over the years. I'd considered studying in the United States, but it was too expensive. I'd tried to date a few American guys (not all at once!), but those relationships all led to nothing. Eventually I realized I had to let go of my teenage dream of moving to the United States, concluding if there was something in it that God would make a way. I buried the sense of knowing in my heart. Then, sixteen years after my first visit, I was standing on American soil and calling it home.

I was in awe of the vast Arizona sky and loved the sparse beauty of the desert and the mountains that spread beyond Phoenix. I loved the raw desert beauty of rocks and cactus. I tolerated the warnings about Arizona wildlife—the scorpions, rattlesnakes, black widow spiders, and brown recluse spiders. I shuddered because it seemed as if there were a thousand ways to die.

Then there was the heat. I loved living in Valley of the Sun, but I was not prepared for Arizona's heat. It was 107 degrees every day for months, and then it got hotter. Even when it cooled, the seasons didn't seem to change. Although in winter the temperatures dropped to the sixty-degree range, it purely provided the opportunity to wear jeans and a sweater! Yet this was my answered prayer; this was the promise God whispered into my adolescent ears. It was meant to be. That was all that mattered, and that would make everything make sense.

I didn't realize that as I started life in the Sonoran Desert, I also entered a wilderness experience. I didn't know that over the next few years, everything I understood about myself, my faith, and my purpose would be tested to the core. And that I would discover that the broken identities and unrealistic expectations I thought I'd left behind were still very much a part of me.

I stepped into a new world, and once the initial thrill of newness wore off, all turned to weariness. Everything was stripped away. I had to learn how to count money differently; I had to learn how to drive on the other side of the road. Every road was unfamiliar, and even the road signs didn't make sense. There was no favorite restaurant, no familiar grocer, no favorite clothing store. The food was different, and even the food that was the same tasted different. I broke down in a store once because I couldn't find a tin of baked beans. That used to be my comfort food, but not anymore.

It has been said that England and the United States are two countries divided by the same language. I had assumed we'd have language in common, but I found myself having to learn American English.

And those were the easy things. Much harder was that friendships were stripped away. I recognized that friends in England were moving on without me; then I remembered that I was the one who had moved. My friends back home were irreplaceable, and yet I knew I wouldn't survive if I didn't make new friends. But how do you do that as an adult with a husband and an overcrowded schedule?

Hardest of all was that I had left behind my family. I thought of my nephews and niece who would grow up without me. I thought of my elders, my mom and my aunties, and though I'd left London years before, I felt their absence. They were my living connection to my Nigerian heritage. Where in Phoenix could I hear warm Yoruba voices, enjoy jollof rice, and relax in the easy familiarity of trusted, loving members of my extended family? Here in my new world, I was seen only as English.

They didn't know my maiden name, Oyeniran, the name that told my story and my history. I was a Saxton now, and that was fine. But I felt somehow disconnected from my own story, my identity. I felt that no one knew my name. At least not my full name.

## PURPOSE IN THE WILDERNESS

> Remember how the LORD your God led you through the wilderness for these forty years, humbling you and testing you to prove your character, and to find out whether or not you would obey his commands. Yes, he humbled you by letting you go hungry and then feeding you with manna, a food previously unknown to you and your ancestors. He did it to teach you that people do not live by bread alone; rather, we live by every word that comes from the mouth of the LORD. (Deuteronomy 8:2–3)

The wilderness experience was more than physical hardship. The season exposed how the Israelites would react under pressure. What they'd rely on when resources were limited. What they would do when the Promised Land was not yet in sight. Would they still find their identity in God and live out their purpose? Would the testing transform them or tear them apart?

God had set the Israelites free and given them a new identity and purpose. Yet the wilderness experience revealed they were still captive to the wounds of the world and the ways of Egypt. It wasn't obvious on the Passover night when the firstborn sons of Egypt were killed. Nor did it come to light as they were escaping Egypt with their own possessions as well as items of value given to them by the Egyptians (see Exodus 3:19–22). It took time beyond the excitement and adrenalin to reveal that, though they were physically free, they remained in chains.

It took the wilderness experience with its battles and the mundane means for survival to reveal the fragility of their faith and the fault lines of their souls. When life did not meet their expectations and when the pressure and pain intensified, or when God's promises required their hard work, the Israelites turned away from whose they were. They decided, "The LORD must hate us" (Deuteronomy 1:27).

They lost sight of their calling, and instead chose to be defined by their past experiences in Egypt, meaning four hundred years of slavery (see Acts 7:6). The culture and values of Egypt were hard to leave behind. Wandering in the wilderness exposed the truth that in order to be fully free, the Israelites didn't just need to get out of Egypt. They needed to get Egypt out of them.

Did the Israelites make their escape? Not exactly. Moses sent a twelve-man reconnaissance squad to explore the Promised Land, to look at the land and the best places for God's people to settle and build new lives. They returned forty days later with rich fruit, supplies, and descriptions of an abundant landscape. But ten of the twelve gave a negative report about people living in the area, stating unequivocally that the Israelites were no match for the inhabitants. "Next to them we felt like grasshoppers, and that's what they thought, too!" (Numbers 13:33).

The Israelites panicked and refused to enter the land. Caleb and Joshua, the two spies who were confident about the mission, begged the people to reconsider. After all, they said, the Lord was their covenant Partner and Protector (see Numbers 13:30; 14:7–9). But the people determined to find a new leader who would take them back to Egypt. It's hard to believe, but when they were offered the Promised Land, the Israelites chose a return to captivity.

In the end, Egypt was not an option. The Israelites returned to a life of wandering in the desert until every last fighting man from the generation that had refused to enter the land had died (see Numbers 14:30–35; Deuteronomy 1:35). The younger generation would see the Promised Land, with Joshua and Caleb leading the way. Until then, God's people would remain in the wilderness. The journey to the land of promise would have lasted no longer than mere weeks if they had trusted God. Instead, it took forty years.

## HUMBLED BY THE WILDERNESS

My husband and I had moved to Phoenix as part of a team serving a church. It was a very different, smaller role compared to what I was used to. Prior to this move, I had served in leadership at my previous church as part of the speaking team. I had planted a college-aged congregation and spoken at conferences. In contrast, this time I was very much a utility player on the team in support of other people, filling in wherever I was needed. It was unexpectedly humbling that no one knew my previous accomplishments.

Add this to the ongoing demands of having to learn a new culture, context, and way forward.

I felt I had entered a foreign world. The team culture was different from what I was used to. I was living my dream, wasn't I? So why did it seem that my voice was less welcome here? Why did I feel the need, at times, to talk about the woman I used to be? Was I just sharing my experiences, or was there something more?

I found myself turning to old survival methods, old patterns of proving myself. I was in the land of promise, following God's call, but I kept looking backward to find my meaning.

What had given me meaning in the past? What had determined my worth? I found myself falling back on former ways:

- I would work twice as hard.
- I would be twice as good.
- I would prove my value.

I wandered my way through, reminding myself that I was fulfilling my destiny.

Chris and I had our children while living in the desert. The doctors said I was having a boy, and we prepared the room accordingly. Then she was born, all girl. Our second girl was born the following year.

Nothing could prepare me for the earthquake of emotion I felt with a newborn baby girl in my arms. Nothing could prepare me for the way my past collided with the present as I cradled the future. It was painful and redemptive all at the same time.

I wanted our daughters to feel safe and secure. Permanent. I was determined to do everything in my power to give them the life they were worthy of. I'd work twice, three times as hard if I needed to.

There was definitely wonder in the wandering. God moves in power in the wilderness. People came to faith in our community. We saw miracles of people healed and marriages transformed. Yet on a personal level, I struggled. When the kids were babies and in preschool, sleep was a rare treat. With sleep in short supply, it was harder for me to pray and read the Bible. It was harder to find the mental margin to fully engage with God. The paths I used to walk down to connect with God didn't work anymore. In England I had loved taking long walks with God. Now in Phoenix, walking in one-hundred-degrees-plus heat meant my walks needed to be shorter for six months of the year.

It was harder to worship and participate in the wider church community with young ones needing nursing, attention, and naps! I was used to being at the center of things at church, now I was unexpectedly left on the edges. Was I really fulfilling my destiny? Was this what I longed to come to the United States for? To sit in sweatpants, covered in spit-up, just to hold my babies? I loved holding my babies, but I could have done that in England and had the benefit of my friends and family nearby. Plus paid maternity leave!

In my twenties, I had learned to use my voice and slay my giants. Having learned those lessons, I expected to feel more confident in my thirties. This was the life I wanted, wasn't it? To get married and have children; to live in the United States. And yet I spent most of my days feeling conflicted and confused; I felt happy yet lost all at the same time.

I knew who I used to be, but I wasn't sure who I was anymore. I didn't look the same. Having children changed my body, and there was no bouncing back to what it was before. I was softer, rounder. My feet even grew a size (because apparently size ten wasn't enough!). My hair changed. But I was fearfully and wonderful made, wasn't I?

I didn't know what I was here for. I had big dreams and I held on to big promises, but it wasn't happening. The dry heat of the Arizona wilderness eroded me.

For all the growth and redemption that'd I'd experienced, the truth I'd known, the giants slain, the cracks in my identity were now being exposed. This looked a lot like my Egypt. I felt insecure, with everything to prove and more. I felt lonely, voiceless, and purposeless. And I sometimes wondered if God still loved me or if He had simply abandoned me in the desert.

## God's Purpose in Your Wilderness

The wilderness can test your identity to the breaking point. It's where the authenticity of your purpose is challenged to its core. The pressure and pain of the experience strips away pretension and reveals what is truly happening inside. It reveals the fault lines of your broken identity, uncovering the expectations that you idolize. It exposes where your heart quietly grew toxic and bitter. It reveals whether your relationship with God is so fragile that you moved away from who and whose you are.

The wilderness confronts you with a clear choice: when you are under pressure, will you exchange longed-for redemption for the old ways of life? Will the wilderness transform you or tear you apart?

Take some time to reflect on your wilderness journey:

- How has your wilderness sojourn tested your sense of identity and purpose?
- What did it expose about the state of your heart and your relationship with God?

In Phoenix, people would speak about monsoon season. I thought it meant rain, refreshing rain. But instead of rain we got spectacular lightning storms or blinding dust storms. In later years, we sometimes would get a haboob: a giant wall of dust created from high winds rushing out of a collapsing thunderstorm. The solid wall of dust would seep through the entire valley, clouding and covering everything in its wake. The wall blocked out the sun, people couldn't drive, and many would have trouble breathing.

> The wilderness can test your identity to the breaking point. It's where the authenticity of your purpose is challenged to its core.

My husband's ordination training required that we spend a year in the Midwest, in Minnesota. So we moved during monsoon season. I thought we'd escaped the dust storms.

What I didn't realize was that regardless of my geographical location, in my wilderness the storms were brewing and building. Another haboob of a different type was forming. It was so big and so violent it swept me into its valley.

I'd lost sight of who I was in the wilderness; I'd be completely undone in the valley.

# 9

# In the Valley

MY SISTER,

I wonder sometimes if the dream feels like a cruel fantasy to you. You lived a dream until it was stolen from you without warning. Then you found your life in ruins.

And now you're supposed to rebuild and dream again? You didn't ask for another dream; you loved the last one. And even if you are open to a new dream, there is the haunting, unnerving feeling that any moment you might be forced to wake up again.

I've heard that grief is a gift, but I've never enjoyed receiving it. The best I can say is that grief has medicinal features. Grief has left me numb, staring into a void, desperately wanting to go back in time. And unable and unwilling to move forward. Grief has confronted me in predictable moments such as at anniversaries, and worse, at unexpected times. My tears were not enough to expel the grief, not enough to heal my broken heart.

Grief crushed my expectations and stole my dreams. And then it took a part of me. My losses redefined my identity in ways I simply wasn't prepared for. My voice and purpose were suddenly deemed irrelevant during bigger, more painful events.

I live with loss just as you *do*. But I still can't imagine what you feel in your unique circumstances. I can't know the pain of the details of your journey. But I see you, kneeling, standing, walking among the ruins. I see you learning a new normal because life gave you no choice. I've seen you search for where the big, long-lost words of *faith, hope,* and *love* will fit. It's never easy.

I cannot give you all the answers, but I can tell you one thing that has carried me through: there is One who is walking in the ruins with you. He bears your sorrows and carries your griefs. This One cares so tenderly that He stores your tears in a bottle. He sees you.

My love, He will not rush you to leave the valley in pursuit of the mountaintop. And He will not leave.

Weeping with you,

Jo

~

Autumn had always been my favorite season, and in Minnesota the breathtaking colors presented a beautiful contrast to the desert hues of Arizona.

Our move hadn't been planned, but it was a necessary part of my husband's training. To finish up as quickly as possible, he'd be in classes and training all day and then studying at night. This was for our future. I'd be in an apartment alone with two children under the age of two, living in an unfamiliar city with no friends or relatives nearby and no ideas of what to do and how to keep two little ones entertained. After our lengthy adjustment to Phoenix, I felt even more vulnerable. My worlds kept slipping away from me. Still it was only for a year; perhaps it could be an adventure?

I needed to carve out a life for us—and fast. I'd never experienced a Minnesota winter, but I had been warned that I would be confined to our apartment . . . for months. Now was the time to get outside. I would get out and be around people even if I didn't know them. The girls needed to look at something other than Elmo and Barney. Heck, I needed something more than Elmo and Barney.

Everyone I met recommended going to Como. There was the zoo, the park, and the lake, and it was free and only a couple of miles away. Como is where our Minnesota adventure began. When the kids proved challenging or simply got bored, I whisked them away to the zoo to stare transfixed at lions and polar bears. We hunted the sloth in the tropical rain forest and stared at flowers in the conservatory. My girls would travel the zoo, taking in the world with their wide, brown eyes. For an afternoon we were explorers, adventurers.

On other days, we'd go for a walk around the lake looking for birds and bugs. I loved Lake Como. To be near the water after life in the desert felt like a personal oasis.

As the temperatures plummeted, we arranged to avoid the worst of the midwestern winter by spending the Christmas holidays and the month of January back in Arizona. The plan was to reconnect with our community and enjoy our friends. Alongside that, it was an opportunity to schedule some key work meetings as we moved toward the future. We'd talked and dreamed with our leaders for months. My husband was going to join the pastoral team. I'd have a part-time role. We'd move nearer to the church and serve young families.

But that winter we returned to Arizona to discover that the doors of opportunity at our church had slammed shut. It was over. We were told they were "moving in a different direction." It didn't matter what had been said and done, the steps we had taken, the training undertaken, the promises that had been made to us. It didn't matter that we'd left our home country only three years before. We were told there were no jobs for us, not now, not in the future.

It's nothing personal, they said. It's never anything personal.

But you know and I know it felt intensely personal, like the worst kind of breakup with a cruel twist: "It's not me, it's you." I felt rejected and betrayed. Worst of all, I felt utterly powerless. The most vulnerable part of it was our visa application. This job was supposed to secure our work visas. Without it, if we didn't find new jobs, we might have to find a new country.

Why had we uprooted our life in England? We had finally made friends and were building our life in the United States, but now I couldn't fathom where we might go next, where we would live, what we would do. Where was God's promise now?

I had turned down exciting opportunities in England to pursue this dream. And for what? For broken promises and discarded dreams? Yes, it felt very personal.

## THE VALLEY OF DRY BONES

One of the greatest prophets of ancient Israel was taken to a valley. He kept a record of his eerie experience: "I was carried away by the

Spirit of the LORD to a valley filled with bones," Ezekiel wrote. "He led me all around among the bones that covered the valley floor. They were scattered everywhere across the ground and were completely dried out" (Ezekiel 37:1–2).

The tour devastated him.

The priest Ezekiel was among the Jews exiled to Babylon in 597 BCE under Nebuchadnezzar's rule. While in exile, God called him to prophesy to his people. For seven years, Ezekiel's words were filled with judgment, telling people that the beloved city of Jerusalem would fall because of their rebellion against God. Eventually his words were proven true.

Jerusalem fell to the Assyrians after the city was under siege for two years. Many of its inhabitants were tortured and killed; many died due to famine and disease brought on by the siege. The survivors were taken to Babylon, and Jerusalem was burned to the ground. Even the Temple, understood to hold God's Word and His presence, was destroyed.

From a great distance, Ezekiel continued to prophesy. Eventually, the tone and content of his prophecies shifted. Now there were words of hope and restoration, relationships and identity, a renewed calling. These were redemptive words.

Then, without warning, the Spirit of God carried Ezekiel into an all-encompassing vision. The priest and prophet was led onto a battlefield in a valley where he was given a vision of war, plunder, and death. God made him face it all. The lasting visual image for most who read his prophecy is the valley floor covered with dried-out bones.

The pattern of Assyrian warfare was that corpses weren't

buried, but rather stripped of their valuables and left exposed for birds and wild animals. This is death beyond death.

The Spirit of God led Ezekiel up and down the vast expanse of the valley, through the picked-over bones. It was irrelevant that contact with the dead made this Hebrew priest unclean. These bones were people he lived among, people he served with at the Temple. Most painfully, perhaps, was this: among the bones were those of his wife, whose loss he couldn't even mourn (see Ezekiel 24). It's no wonder, then, that alongside the devastating vision the Hebrew idioms used is the language of lament.

Ezekiel's language recorded in this part of his prophecy mirrors a psalm of communal lament. In Hebrew literature at that time, bones represented being at the very end of yourself, echoing an overwhelmed and anguished soul.

The exiled people of Israel were traumatized by the attack on their city. And a priest had lost his freedom, his wife, his city, his community, his role. It wasn't supposed to be like this.

Only a vision of a valley this overwhelming could begin to capture the vast expanse of trauma and sorrow. It was grief upon grief.

## BONES UNDER BONES

Arizona, with its beautiful blue skies and its warm winter sun, now felt like the coldest place on earth. The rugged desert was cruel and threatening, a desolate howling wilderness. I didn't know where my next home might be. The disorienting feeling of rootlessness scared me. I felt temporary. The feeling was reminiscent of the year following my removal from foster care, when I left my foster mother. Except this time, it wasn't just me who was affected. I had a husband and two young children. Now the rootlessness might touch my children's lives too.

We returned to Minnesota, unexpectedly grateful to be away from it all. We did all we knew how to do by just carrying on. Chris returned to classes and homework. The girls and I stayed in our apartment with Barney and Elmo and *WordWorld*. It was back to days of rummaging through the dressing-up box and snack times with sippy cups and Cheerios. Occasionally we'd spend thirty minutes dressing up in winter gear to go spend two minutes outside before the girls asked to go back inside. It was much easier to watch the winter from our apartment window.

I needed time and space to process what had happened. However, the girls' nap times were not long enough—there was always something else to do, to be cleaned, and to be prepared. The apartment felt too confining. When Chris had some downtime during the day, I went out alone. This time I went to Lake Como.

The leaves had abandoned the trees; the birds had long ago left in search of warmer, friendlier climes. The landscape was white, and the sky was gray and heavy. I stood in borrowed winter clothing staring at the ice covering the lake, shocked and bruised. Life had changed and I felt powerless. I stared at the frozen lake and waited.

These were only the first scattering of bones on the valley floor.

Four weeks later, a light quietly went out. It had been fading for some time, but for as long as it was there, it lit my way. Then, silently, it went dark. May, my foster mother, had passed away. She was 102 years old. Her passionate heart had finally worn her body out.

I had lost the light in my childhood. May represented security and safety. She was mine and I was hers. She was there when I needed her, but not anymore. I had thought that I would know in my heart when she died. I thought it would be like one of those movies where the protagonist suddenly sits upright, feeling and knowing that life has passed. But I didn't know, and I felt guilty and robbed at the same time.

In a final, selfless gesture, May had sent word to make sure my brother and I received her goodbye. When I called my brother to tell him the news, I felt like we were children again. I was taken back to the time when I was four or five years old and he was nine or ten, both of us navigating our way through a world too big for us. When I was a little girl, May was my summer. She was the moon and the stars. Now, I couldn't imagine a world without her.

At Lake Como, I stood in the cold and the wind. I watched and waited.

The sorrow of having lost May would not soon pass. But only five weeks later, my father died. My father, the one who had defined my life by his absence. The one I looked like, from whom I inherited my height, my personality, my eyes, and my ridiculously long, flat feet. The one whose presence I had longed for throughout my youth. The man I had loved and hated in the same breath, because, despite everything, he mattered to me. He was mine and I desperately wanted to be his.

My father and I had struggled to connect throughout my life. Even the moments when he made me laugh or smile, I wouldn't let him see me enjoying his wit, his personality. It was as though I didn't want him to know I could forgive him that easily and love him regardless. Still, over the years, we found a way, our way, to build toward a relationship. It was tiring, it was complex, and that was us. It was necessary.

Only two weeks before he left this life, we had our miracle—more than twenty years in the making. We talked, he cried, and we made our peace. There was reconciliation, a healing, and freedom. Now past sins were absolved and a future lay ahead of us. There was hope. We could start over. Then death stole into his room one night and with a stroke took him away. He was gone.

So was I. I was numb and alone on the banks of Lake Como in April. April is supposed to mean spring, but the meteorologists reported this was an extended winter.

I stared at the frozen lake, not able to comprehend my losses. I was thirty-four years old, and two of my parents had died in the space of five weeks. I don't remember crying. I just carried on in the fog of a baby and a preschooler, of career plans derailed and pioneering dreams stalled. Of hopes that were snatched away because it was too late; of natural, inevitable goodbyes that nonetheless shattered my soul. There were days I felt nothing because every pore of my being felt everything and somehow the kindness of the body protected me from what the lack of feeling meant.

Whenever I could, I went to Como. Not to the zoo, not to the conservatory. Just to the lake. I stood and watched and waited.

The weather was overcast and cold. Bitter even. It was the longest winter in years, breaking records that only the meteorologists were interested in. I had never encountered such a brutal, relentless winter. It was too cold to stand outside. Nonetheless, I stood outside a lot because it matched my life. It seemed that just as I'd stagger to my feet, I'd get knocked down again. And again. This time the bullies were too big for me.

It was as though my entire life were under siege. Some of my most significant relationships had been stolen, never to return. My career plans razed. My life stripped away, my dreams plundered, the scabs ripped away until there was only a raw, unhealed wound left. I was at the end of my very self.

All of me was lifeless, little more than dry bones and a deep, aching lament.

Though I'm a hardwired extrovert, my heart felt too tender to share with anyone. Besides, who would I talk to? Friends and family were far away, and Arizona didn't feel safe. We hadn't invested in relationships in Minnesota because we weren't planning to stay long. It felt too hard to share these life-shattering things among the few temporary relationships we had begun.

But suddenly I felt like I had too much to say, too much pain. I couldn't find the words to shape them into something that even I could understand, let alone anyone else. I couldn't risk feeling offended by an accidentally misplaced word or undone by a genuine hug. I think that's why I ended up at the lake even on the coldest days. It was my place of loss and lament:

*I can never speak to my dad again. Just when our relationship was beginning in earnest, we ran out of time. I will never speak to*

*him again. My children will never know him. I will never see him
again.*

*And my Aunty May. She was everything. I'm scared I will
forget her voice, forget how she lived and how she loved me. I don't
want to forget her.*

Finally, I started to talk to God. *I thought You wanted us to
live here. I thought You called us here. Why did You bring us here
if it was going to be like this?*

*Had I been wrong when I felt I was called to America? Or worse,
was it just some fantasy idea that I'd decided was a divine calling?*

*Who did I think I was?*

*It has been so hard and we've tried so hard . . .*

*I don't know where I belong anymore.*

*I don't know what to dream now.*

*I don't know who I am now. I've not known for years.*

Sometimes the prayers sounded like arguments and grief and
loss. I heard them through the numbness as I watched my winter
breath. Sometimes the words made it only as far as my heart.
Some days they were spoken through tears. Sometimes it was simply a frozen lament. At all times, God was there, walking through
my valley of dry bones. Stopping with me to bear witness to each
bone under bone. When grief left me gasping, He was my air.

I know you have experienced the valley of bones, and possibly more than once. No one wants to be taken to the valley,
but once there it's important that we not miss the significance of
Ezekiel's experience. If you're familiar with the story, you'll remember that God ultimately breathed new life into the valley.
Out of the devastation and loss came new life and new purpose for

God's people. It was so miraculous and incredible that it's easy to miss the significance. The Spirit of God walked with Ezekiel in the valley and confronted the priest with the extent of his devastating loss. God led Ezekiel back and forth along the valley floor, uncovering everything, making sure everything had been stripped away. He was with Ezekiel in the ruins of his life. God stood with him in grief.

Where are you in the valley? Take time to reflect on your own life.

- A dream job that didn't materialize.
- A promotion that was yours until it wasn't.
- The end of a relationship.
- The end of a working partnership. It was explained that it wasn't personal, but it feels acutely so.
- An event that tore at the very fabric of your community.
- An entire people lost, exiled, vulnerable to the whims and the ways of another nation, another system.

Maybe for you, like it was for Ezekiel, it's not just what happened, but also the loved ones you have lost. You can no longer see or talk with someone who was everything to you.

Christie longed for love and commitment and marriage. Leslie longed for children instead of the label "infertility." Where has life left you broken with longing? What lies at the bottom of your valley? What are the dry bones that bring you to the end of your deepest self?

How has life in the valley shaped or redefined who you are and how you view your life?

## You're in the Valley. What Happens Now?

The wilderness and the valley are the hardest places to explore. They often jar or even redefine our sense of identity and purpose. We're too crushed to feel known and loved; we are convinced we have nothing left to offer as a voice or a purpose. There are chapters in our redemption journey that feel awful, that *are* awful. We're at the end of ourselves; we are forced to face what life has done to us.

It's tempting to mute our pain rather than face it. Facing it squarely seems like the thing that finally will overwhelm us. We're just barely hanging on, so how could we ever confront the bone piles that might well tip over and bury us? In these places, it often is easier to default to our old ways of coping, to push the gnawing reality of our broken identity aside. We might even attempt to silence the voices that shout pain and loss and loss of identity rather than uncover them, as God did for Ezekiel in the valley.

The wilderness and the valley are the hardest places to explore. They often jar or even redefine our sense of identity and purpose.

We might turn to old habits and try to eat away the pain, or drink it away, or shop too much, work longer and longer hours, sleep when we don't need sleep.

None of those escape attempts work. We have to go to the valley and encounter the dry bones. We need to stay with God there and allow Him to help us face the bones of our lives and identity. It's still a redemption journey, whether we're in a valley or seeing things from a mountaintop.

As I stood month after month beside a frozen lake in Minnesota, I discovered God would help me face my trauma and pain. The same God who took Ezekiel, priest and prophet, into the valley was there with me.

He didn't rush me. He did not expect me to quickly "move on" to new life and exciting things, to "get over" what I'd experienced. He did not consider me faithless or weak for grieving. He was big enough to hear my sorrow and pain, even my anger directed at Him. He did not need me to be happy; He did not need me to be optimistic.

Further, I discovered that He also had helped me face the imprint the losses had left on my soul. It was necessary to read the marks and to understand what each loss was awakening within me.

What were the patterns that still needed healing? God was bringing resurrection, but it started with facing death. He was bringing redemption, but it started by facing all I'd lost.

He wanted to be with me in the valley of bones, and He helped me to face it all.

There are the times when we need to give ourselves permission to lament our dry bones in the depths of our darkest, coldest winter. None of us wants to go to that place, but once there, God is present with us. And even though we can't see it or feel it, He is still moving.

# Breaking Up with Perfection

HEY, LOVE,

I see you, girl, and you are beyond tired. You hit exhaustion some time ago. But you're still going. Your schedule is packed full of commitments you wish you hadn't agreed to, but the *yes* came before common sense had a chance to refuse.

If it were just your schedule, we could talk about time management and then move on. It's not only that there is no time for you. Life gets full. But your mind is full, and there's no space to think or process, so things keep you up at night. You are calculating all that you missed. You are distracted from the present moment.

Your heart is worn because no one is looking out for you the way that you look out for them. That hurts too.

You are weary. Your body tries to tell you about the state of your entire being. You are burning out from trying so hard to prove yourself, but why? There are so many reasons it's hard to narrow them down.

You *still* feel that you have to be Wonder Woman in order to be worthy. Everything you do has to achieve the extraordinary, as though purpose is earned. And because you don't know your name, or you've lost your voice, or because you're uncertain of God's love.

It could well be because you look in the mirror and dislike what you see. Or because your fears tower over you, or that this is not the life you expected and you feel conflicted every day.

To slow down would mean you would have to feel life's losses, and you're scared those feelings would drown you. There are too many feelings now. There is no time to manage them.

It's what we all do with our broken identities: we simply try harder, work harder. We carry wounds, yet we carry on until life forces us to change.

Sometimes it's through a health crisis or divorce or kids leaving home. Sometimes it happens quietly when you feel that you're crumbling on the inside.

Sister, you need to carve out time for soul work. And not just time but also space in your mind and heart. Not because you're bad, but because you are worthy. And we both know that in the early hours of the morning when insomnia rules and your heart is vulnerable, you want to live a different way.

It's hard to let go when you have carried so much for so long, but I'd like to propose an alternative. What could it look like to let Jesus carry you?

Wishing you a restored soul and a thousand naps,

Jo

જી

Years passed in a blink. We'd been living in the United States for a decade, a quarter of my life. New jobs brought new locations and homes. And with them new excitement, new pressures, and new disappointments.

When our children were born here, I felt roots dig into American soil. The roots deepened as our girls grew, made friends, started school. I could no longer describe the United States casually, as "our great adventure." It was no longer an experiment; it was permanent now. So why didn't I feel that way?

I thought often of my family and friends in England. I missed them more after ten years than I did at three or five or seven years, because life had moved on and there was no going back. Time was changing the very fabric of my family. The elders in my family had grown older and frailer. My siblings and I spanned the globe, and our time together was sporadic, always too brief for me. My nephews and my niece were adults now.

As for my friends, I recalled the rites of passage in our lives that we didn't get to share: weddings, children, milestone birthdays, struggles and trials, funerals. Where had the time gone? Did I get the life that I came for?

Was all this worth it? I determined to make it worth it. The identity that always emerged under pressure, my default survival mode, rose again. I'd work twice as hard, three times as hard if necessary, to make it worth it.

That said, after the wilderness and the valley, I wasn't the same person anymore. Those years had worn down my confidence and stunted my boldness. They'd left me acutely aware that I could not control life's outcomes, no matter how hard I tried. If life would knock me down with a disappointment, a bad day, a rough week—I'd get back up again, but slower each time. I was weary. Still, I worked even harder: parenting to working to everything else. I kept myself busy, which had afforded me recognition and approval before. Why wouldn't it do the same again?

But what happens when busy is not just activity but the way you think and the way you feel all the time? You are constantly striving, constantly proving. Eventually it costs you your identity and your purpose. As Alli Worthington notes in her book *Breaking Busy,* "All this busyness, in the end, keeps us just out of reach of the life we were created to live."[1]

I'd forgotten my own name and covered it with the bandage of busy. It's really not hard to do with kids and work. That is, until the tiredness weighed me down.

## Tired of Proving, Tired of Striving, Tired of the Burden

I wonder how He felt when He saw the crushing disappointment on people's faces. I imagine the weight of their stories reflected in their postures. Maybe the people's heartache hung in the air, like a coming storm.

Jesus was watching them. The people were seen by God in the flesh. He knew their journey because God had walked it with them, before them, and after them. Jesus, who had come to earth to save a sinful and broken humanity, knew exactly the burdens that threatened to crush the life out of the people. He was the only One who could transform their lives. The only One who could redeem all that had been and make all things new.

The ancient Israelites lived in a homeland free of foreign rule for only a short period of Israel's history. Israel divided into two kingdoms after Solomon's rule. In time, both kingdoms were invaded, conquered, and taken away into exile. Foreigners were imported to live in the land that had been promised to God's people. And when Jews were allowed to return from exile to rebuild the Temple and the city of Jerusalem, they still did not enjoy peace.

In the first century CE when Jesus lived in Galilee, Palestine suffered under the oppressive footprint of Roman rule. The Jews longed for the promise that God had given through the prophets, generations before. A Messiah would come—the Anointed One. He would overthrow evil and reign. The promise captured the longings of the people, but its fulfillment seemed so distant. It felt like heaven had been silent for hundreds of years.

As for their faith? The Pharisees were religious overachievers who had missed the point. They recognized that when God's people had walked away from God's law, they lost their land and went into exile. The Pharisees were determined to keep this from happening again, so they added rules and regulations to prevent people from breaking rules and producing more bad consequences. They added extra rules to define what it meant to follow God, and people who didn't go along were considered outsiders. What began as Ten Commandments had been expanded to more than *six hundred* rules. Yet no one—not even the most scrupulous rule follower—was any closer to a relationship with the living God.

It's no wonder that Jesus's presence was a lightning strike. He had a completely different posture from anything the people had seen before. He was so secure in God's love that He knew God as Abba . . . *Daddy*. Can you imagine? He was not conflicted or confused; He knew what His life meant and what He was to do with it. He was not crushed by the world; He was free enough to love it. He was empowered by a different and a greater Source than mere Roman rule.

When people encountered Jesus, they were overwhelmed by His love. They'd never seen such power in love, such miracles, such compassion. They'd not encountered such authority. Demons ran in the opposite direction. Even the wind and the waves couldn't control Him. His teaching flowed like fresh, clean water bringing growth to arid ground. People who had dried out were given life again.

## WHERE HAVE YOU BEEN DEFINED
## BY PROVING AND STRIVING?

Jesus said, "Come to me, all of you who are weary and carry heavy burdens, and I will give you rest. Take my yoke upon you. Let me teach you, because I am humble and gentle at heart, and you will find rest for your souls. For my yoke is easy to bear, and the burden I give you is light" (Matthew 11:28–30).

I'm comforted that Jesus spoke those words to other misguided people with dreams of what freedom should look like. The ancient Jews sought a Davidic figure, a conquering king who would rout the Romans and restore Israel. And while Jesus confirmed that He, indeed, was the promised conquering King, He was a serious disappointment as leader of the rebellion.

The promised Messiah, having arrived and begun doing his kingly work, was making all things new, working His purposes for all of creation. And beyond anyone's wildest dreams, He was inviting the *people* to participate. He invites us, you and me, to join in.

"Come to me, all of you who are weary."

Jesus wasn't speaking only about a tired moment or a long day. He extended an invitation to *everyone* who was dragged down by a chronically weary life. The Jews of that era were in a place of always trying but never reaching; always pushing, driving, and striving yet never arriving. Israel was occupied territory, so even though the people lived in the area of the Promised Land, they were never fully free.

*Come. To. Me.* Jesus offered close relationship, a warm and radical alternative to the broken system of the religious leaders who had elevated themselves and their rules.

*I will give you rest.* Jesus took the loving initiative in the relationship, just as a covenant partner would. And He offered the people something they desperately needed: rest. Instead of shame and blame, instead of endless striving, instead of relentless pressure to achieve and prove themselves, what Jesus offered was rest. Yet the type of rest He offered was deeper than an end to activity. The word for *rest* here also meant "comfort and calm, refreshment, and an opportunity to recover your strength." Jesus offered the kind of rest that would give the people back their lives.

How could this Rabbi offer such an unattainable dream? Jesus provided more details.

"Take my yoke upon you and learn from me, for I am gentle and humble in heart, and you will find rest for your souls. For my yoke is easy and my burden is light" (Matthew 11:29–30, NIV).

In the Bible, the word *yoke* often symbolized servanthood and submission, burden, even slavery. The Pharisees called people to carry the "yoke of the Torah."[2] They spoke of the yoke of the law, the yoke of the commandments, the yoke of the kingdom, and the yoke of God.

In order to plow fields effectively, oxen were harnessed in teams to a yoke, a piece of wood hewn to fit the oxen so that the burden of pulling a plow would not chafe them. The oxen would plow for hours at a time, so a young, feisty ox was harnessed alongside an older, experienced one. That way, the younger animal would learn how to navigate the field and how to pace itself in order to maintain energy for an entire day. It must have looked bizarre from a distance, the strong experienced ox alongside a young bullock. In reality, the older, experienced ox was carrying the burden, pulling the weight. But the younger animal was learning how to do its job.

Jesus used the image of a yoke to invite the people into the kind of close relationship with Him where He is the experienced leader, pulling the weight, carrying the burden, and tethered to *us*. Ultimately, He carries the burdens of all our sin, guilt, shame, and brokenness all the way to the Cross. Instead of standing *over* us, He promises to remain alongside us as we plow through the rugged landscape of our lives.

Jesus's promise, which dates back two thousand years, has not changed. He treats us in a way we will never be treated by the world around us. He has shown Himself to be gentle, humble, loving. When people are yoked to Jesus, they find freedom from rules, requirements, and judgment. This is the place where we can finally learn how to live. He invites us to live with Him, paired closely to Him, linked to who He is and the work He is doing. We are invited to learn, to find out how to live and navigate our way through this conflicted, broken world.

> In Jesus, we no longer have to weary ourselves
> in the busyness that seeks to prove our worth.

Many days this seems impossible. But Jesus continues to say, "Come and learn at My side." The yoke Jesus offers is not oppressive. The people did not find rest under the expectation of the Pharisees and their harsh system. In contrast, Jesus's yoke is custom made for His people. It fits just right and is fully suited to the lives we live.

In Jesus, we no longer have to weary ourselves in the busyness that seeks to prove our worth. In Jesus, our exhausted minds and empty souls can finally discover a place of rest. And there with Him we can recover the life we were meant to live.

## COME TO ME . . .

He first said it to me through a girl in my elementary-school class who invited me to church. During Sunday school, Jesus said, "Come to me." I had just then, for the first time, heard His story.

I realize now He has been saying "Come to me" throughout

my life. He said it in the crowded sanctuary of an Anglican church as a woman prophesied and told me whose I was. He said it when I wept in front of a mirror, wondering if I ever would be enough. Even when He taught me how to slay giants, it was an invitation to walk with Him through the obstacles that stood in our way. At times, it has been hard to hear His invitation.

I couldn't hear Him easily in the Arizona desert, and I was numbed by grief when I stood at the lake, freezing in Minnesota. As the years passed, I couldn't hear Him because of the noise of a busy life and my overcrowded mind. And for a while, I wouldn't hear Him simply because, after all this time, I was still trying to be twice as good at life in order to be good enough for the world around me. I could not hang up those red boots. Some broken identities are harder to let go than others, especially the ones that really worked for you in the distant past.

Eventually the cracks began to show in my life. I'd end up at the doctor's office seeking help for stress-related ailments. I wondered if I could ever switch off my mind so I could sleep at night. I seemed to live with constant anxiety. The cracks also showed up in the way I'd first lose myself in endless work, then lose myself in endless, mind-numbing television. And in the way that sometimes, in the earliest hours of the morning in a rare moment of vulnerability, I'd whisper in prayer that I wanted a break from how I felt.

I finally heard Jesus one day when I read His invitation to come. It wasn't the first time I'd read the words. But they seemed to be lit in neon for days on end. Jesus noted my nocturnal whispers and spoke to my life, my mind, and my soul. And in the invitation, He spoke to everything that lay behind the busyness.

He saw where my heart remained scarred, my foundations weak. He knew the brokenness that still attempted to take away my true name. He saw patterns of behavior that drive my choices: the fear that I'll never truly belong, that I'm *temporary*. The hesitation I feel when I have a new idea or plan, a big dream that I need to share but fear I will be rejected or minimized. Would I give in to these things, make myself small, keep my passions to myself in order to feel safe? Or would I dare to believe that, yoked with Jesus right next to me, I could do this? Jesus saw me and heard me when I was cringing in anticipation of once again ending up bruised on life's playground.

He saw the wounds that most define me: overachievement and perfectionism. I was convinced I had to be Wonder Woman to fit in, to be worthy. He knew that I've worn that chain like a charm bracelet for decades, adding to its weight. He saw me fighting every systemic *ought* and cultural *should*. He saw me exhausting myself working to prove I was worthy in spaces that use only the measurements of "not enough" or "too much" when it came to my body, my womanhood, my parenting, my abilities, my calling, my work, my beauty—even my British accent, my African heritage, and my black skin.

Survival is not the same as being whole.

He saw where I had felt validated and justified, even successful, when perfectionism had worked for me in a world that honors overwork and overachievement. And He had seen where all this had hurt me. Where it had wounded relationships, violated my body, stunted creativity, singed my faith. Survival is not the same as being whole.

> *Come to Me, He said. I loved you unconditionally long before you even knew My name.*
>
> *Come to Me. I will never leave you. I will walk with you. I will be with you.*
>
> *Learn from Me, He said. I know how you feel you have to keep plowing through the fields of your life. I know the terrain, the different seasons. I am paired with you in the yoke. You no longer have to prove you are the strongest, the best, the hardest working.*
>
> *Stay close to Me and learn from Me, the real Me.*
>
> *Let Me disciple you in a new way of life. Where you don't spend yourself in pursuit of the world's approval and lose your soul along the way.*
>
> *Let Me disciple you where you are fully known. Where black was always beautiful. Where African was always able.*
>
> *Take My yoke and know you already are worthy. You are a woman with a contribution to make to the world regardless of anyone else's approval. Where your voice was designed to be heard and fully ready to lead the way. Where the yoke fits, custom made for you.*
>
> *It still will be hard; it will be challenging. Some soil is harder, and it will be difficult to break through the ground. Sometimes you will feel the sun's brutal heat, and you will want to turn away. But learn from Me so you*

*won't get distracted or disillusioned. Learn from Me by*
*walking beside Me.*

Could I exchange the oppressive yoke of the world for one
that fits, learning from the stronger Ox? Would I finally let go of
my need to be a version of Wonder Woman to survive my story?
Would I realize that she could never overpower the oppressors but
Jesus can and does?

> Are you ready to say goodbye to
> the overly committed, overly
> busy life that falsely promises to
> affirm your identity?

Was I finally ready to hang up my red boots? Are you? Are
you ready to say goodbye to the overly committed, overly busy life
that falsely promises to affirm your identity? Are you ready to
confront your brokenness, rather than keep hiding it underneath
greater efforts to prove yourself to others?

## Take His Yoke; Lay Yours Down

"Come to me" is the Savior's gracious initiation. But it's also a call
to surrender. We can't pick up His yoke if we're still wearing an old
one. It's a call to yield our entire selves—all the broken pieces,
every weary burdened bone—to Jesus once again. Jesus invites us
to learn in relationship rather than achieving more and more in
hopes of gaining someone's approval.

For me, surrender looked like an act of faith to finally turn my back on my Egypt and to walk into the Promised Land.

Dear Overachievement,

I'm breaking up with you. I have another calling and another Partner. I'm now part of what my Redeemer is doing in the world.

It's over.

Jo

He's worth it. He redeems the life I've had, He breaks every single chain, and He leads me forward, including me on His team to renew the world. This is how I want to live. This is how daily I choose to live. This is how I am learning to live with every step I take.

## STEPS TOWARD RECOVERING YOUR LIFE

"Are you tired? Worn out? Burned out on religion? Come to me. Get away with me and you'll recover your life. I'll show you how to take a real rest. Walk with me and work with me—watch how I do it. Learn the unforced rhythms of grace. I won't lay anything heavy or ill-fitting on you. Keep company with me and you'll learn to live freely and lightly" (Matthew 11:28–30, MSG).

We've covered a lot of ground. We have recognized that though God gave us identity and purpose, our experiences and environment have distracted us, have at times damaged us, and have done their best to derail us.

Wherever you are, whatever the conflicts in your journey, Jesus offers you an invitation. Go back to the passage that captures His invitation to you, Matthew 11:28–30. Read the passage a few times. Which words light up in neon for you? How is God speaking to you?

Next, take time to bring your story to Him. Come to Him with all that has wrongly named you, all that has defined you. Bring Him your weary wilderness and all that it has exposed in you. Don't forget to bring Him your dry bones. Talk to Him about what's really behind the busyness that has burned you out.

Finally, consider what it is that you need to surrender so you can move forward. In which areas is the busyness of your life more than a simple matter of a full calendar? Where is your busyness a failed attempt to fill empty spaces in your life?

Reflect on what it could look like to yield yourself fully to Jesus. Is there a broken identity you've held on to more tightly than others? What do you need to break up with? Write a letter if you need to. Write a letter even if you might not need to, to help you clarify what might be calling for your attention.

Now that you have surrendered the old yoke—the one that broke you—it's time to recover your life. Now is the time to start living the life you were made for. The next few chapters offer suggestions to help you on your way.

# The Song in My Heart

Hey, Sister,

I've been your companion for a while now, but while letters and books are fun, they're no replacement for the flesh-and-blood experience of walking through life with someone. So who will be your companions for the next leg of the journey? You'll need people who see you and know you, people unafraid to remind you of the fullness of who you are. They won't be threatened by you because they are the kind of women who celebrate who you are. You need people who *want* to hear your voice and don't mind how loud it gets. People who get excited about your dreams and your unfolding purpose. Has anyone (other than Jesus!) come to mind yet?

I understand your concerns. The reality is that people can cause great pain in our lives. They have named and shamed us; they have bullied, belittled, and silenced us. They have rejected us and hurt us in unimaginable ways. It has taken us years to emerge from the wreckage of broken relationships. It's hard to trust people now.

So how could you possibly invite anyone into this experience with you? It has been so tender in places that including another seems like the worst place to risk such vulnerability.

Yet there is another truth that we should acknowledge: people have been some of the greatest instruments of healing and redemption in our lives. They have blessed us and built us, they have listened and identified with us. They have stood with us and invested in us. They have befriended us and loved us and then loved us more. They have seen us and empowered us.

Brené Brown has noted, in her book *Daring Greatly,* "We're hardwired for connection—it's what gives purpose and meaning to our lives."[1]

God's Dream of You includes His dream for a redemptive covenant community. The kind of environment where we don't just attend, we belong. Where we don't solely observe, but we engage as we share our journey by sharing lives and stories.

Still unconvinced? That's okay.

When we've been wounded by the bad, it's hard to even image the possibilities of the good. But the good does exist. So to help you move toward it (and tentatively is fine!), let me share a vision of the good. This is the kind of good that God can do when He transforms us through community.

For you always,

Jo

Remember Naomi?

Naomi had been away from her hometown for decades. She and her family had left home because of famine to settle in the Gentile land of Moab. A new beginning in a foreign land turned to tragedy when her husband, Elimelech, died. Her sons also died after living ten years in the foreign nation. Widowed and without her sons, the woman Naomi was very different from the girl who had left her hometown.

But alone and without family support, where could she go? Having heard that God was providing food for people in the land she had left, she set off on the long journey back. She encouraged her Moabite daughters-in-law to return to their own families. Maybe they would have a second chance at security and happiness. Weeping, Orpah went back to her family. But Ruth refused to leave Naomi on her own. They arrived together in Bethlehem.

The Naomi who returned home had been renamed by the tragedies she had experienced. While her original name, Naomi, still meant "pleasant," she had renamed herself Mara, meaning "bitter." She even told the townspeople to refer to her as Mara (see Ruth 1:19–21).

In this ancient culture, two women alone were extremely vulnerable. Many widows were forced to turn to prostitution in order to survive. Naomi was back home but without a husband or sons to support her. In addition to their overwhelming grief, she and Ruth had none of the legal or economic protection that men would have afforded them. And to further complicate their circumstances, Ruth was a Moabitess. The people of Bethlehem were foreign to her, and she was a foreigner in this new place. Between Judah and Moab was a history of antagonism and contempt. Would Ruth ever be accepted, or would she be maligned and possibly abused because of her ethnicity?

As the story unfolds, we see restoration for both Ruth and Naomi. Ruth is welcomed and given leftover grain in a field, which coincidentally was owned by Boaz, one of Naomi's close male relatives. Boaz found his place in Jewish and Christian theology as an archetype of the guardian-redeemer. According to Jewish law, the role of guardian-redeemer was multidimensional, designed to protect the interests of extended family members. Initially Boaz offered protection, encouragement, and extra supplies for Ruth and Naomi (see Ruth 2:8–9, 14–15). But after Ruth's bold and hard-to-resist marriage proposal, Boaz worked even more on Ruth and Naomi's behalf. He legally became their guardian-redeemer, ensuring their protection and providing hope for the future. As part of the deal, Boaz accepted Ruth's overtures and they were married. Together Boaz and Ruth had a son.

The book of Ruth ends with Naomi reclaiming her first name. No longer bitter, she was once again safe and secure, her life renewed, surrounded by family and with a grandson on her lap. Ruth had fully integrated into her community, and her son would become King David's grandfather. Ruth found herself in the rich ancestral line of kings and ultimately the lineage of the King of kings.

God still works in exactly this way.

## Voices That Bring Us Home

It had been a full week with multiple flights, multiple hotels, and more than a few speaking engagements. After landing in Washington, DC, I picked up a rental car and began navigating city traffic to get to the next event. I was nervous and tense. It was an unfamiliar car, the GPS was slow, and I felt overwhelmed as I worked my way through horrible traffic and around the occasional crazy pedestrian. *Stupid car,* I thought. If it had been a Toyota, it would have been easy. I know Toyotas.

Finally, I disconnected my phone and pressed a few buttons until I landed on a radio station. And that is when the soundtrack of my youth filled the car. Parliament and the sound of funk made my shoulders relax, just a little. Then Prince sang about a little red Corvette, and I remembered how I fell in love with his genre-defying sound. Stevie Wonder began to sing "Sir Duke," and I broke into a smile, remembering how my husband, Chris, and I made the impulsive decision to book tickets to see Stevie on our previous wedding anniversary. We lined up like excited school kids with thousands of other fans to spend three hours in the presence of a musical genius. I danced in the arena aisles, happy and free.

Meanwhile, back in DC traffic, Evelyn King's "Love Come Down" sent me straight back to the early eighties and immediately I was at home, enviously watching my siblings getting ready to go out for an evening with friends. I determined that one day that would be me. I could still recall every word and every note of the song thirty years on.

I soon was so immersed in the music that my anxiety had gone. Every song told my story and was a calming gift to me.

Loose Ends's song "Slow Down" took me back to my teens, desperate to wear cool clothes and know all the dance moves like the popular girls. Some girls at school had beautiful Jheri curls or relaxed hair. My cornrows felt so immature in comparison. We were all changing so fast that our emotions couldn't keep up. At twelve we all had read Judy Blume's *Are You There, God? It's Me, Margaret* because she seemed to share our angst. By age fourteen we'd moved on to *Forever . . .*, passing the book to one another as if it were seditious literature. Then I was reading Maya Angelou and Shakespeare and watching Oprah on television. I was desperate to be older and wiser. To be pretty and liked. To not feel so awkward and uncertain.

As I struggled through traffic, I smiled, grateful for the painful adolescent memories, realizing I had turned out okay. I was at a stoplight when Earth, Wind & Fire's "September" came on the radio, but it didn't stop me from dancing. I *may* have held up a number of drivers when the light changed. Finally, Chaka Khan belted out "Ain't Nobody," and I was reminded of my sisterhood of friends. In my twenties, at weddings and parties, it was the song we would kind of lose ourselves to. We'd dance together and laugh, and yet we would each be lost in our own story as we moved.

When I reached my destination, I circled the church's parking lot a few times until the song was finished. I mean, it was Chaka Khan. I wasn't tense anymore; I was breathing deeply and smiling broadly. Yet I felt if I heard another song from my past I'd burst into tears. You've been there, right?

The conference organizers gifted me with an appointment with a makeup artist, Sade. She's a Nigerian like me and had spent her youth and early adult years in London like me. Now Sade was building a life in the United States. Within minutes we were talking like sisters. In fact, she reminded me of my sister Catherine, with the same warm lilt in her voice that hinted at a playful, quirky side. And like Catherine she was deep, possessing a kind of proverbial wisdom that spoke of insights hard won.

Sade and I had walked similar paths in life. We had walked down the same streets in London, eaten the same food. We laughed fondly over how our parents' generation wanted us to be lawyers and doctors, leaders in serious professions. And how many of us studied economics and business and finance. Art was a hobby, and yet here we were living lives that were definitely off script. We laughed, remembering our elders fondly, not defiantly. I wondered if maybe now, as a second-time immigrant myself, I understood my mom's and aunties' dreams for me. Maybe now I could interpret their intensity more fully. Perhaps my voice carries the same sense of urgency as I try to communicate hope, sheer sacrifice, and hard work to my daughters.

There were flags around the church sanctuary indicating the nations represented in the congregation. I found the Union Jack and kept searching, searching until my eyes beheld the Nigerian flag, and I could not stop smiling. At some point I greeted the Nigerians in the audience, and there was a loud cheer. I felt a unique kind of welcome. Throughout the weekend I met Brits, Nigerians, and even Nigerian Brits like me. I realized that I held each hand a little longer. I smiled more fully, drinking in every moment. I basked in the beauty of their skin and their hairstyles and their clothing and the cadence of their speech that hinted at every place they had lived. I don't speak Yoruba, but even hearing it again moved me deeply. I heard my distant family. And for the first time in a very long time, "me" felt like "we." We'd all be together for only this short window of time, but knowing they were also in the United States made me feel a little less *other* and a little less lonely.

## God's Extended Family

It's easy to assume that establishing and recovering our identity and purpose are individual pursuits, or that doing these things is something just between us and God. But it's important to remember that God is relational in His very being and nature. He is Father, Son, and Spirit, and He has designed us with community in mind. Humanity was never designed to function as isolated individuals (see Genesis 2), and the covenant relationship with God included a covenant community.

When Jesus taught His disciples how to pray, He invited them to begin with "Our Father" (Matthew 6:9). Those two words remind us that He is not just *my* Father, He is *ours*. We are part of a wider community. Furthermore, because He is our *Father,* we're reminded that this community is more than a religious club; it's a family. The biblical expression of family is not limited to the relatively recent Western ideal of the nuclear family. Rather, it is an extended family that embraces both blood and nonblood ties. The family that is the covenant community becomes the context for covenant love in action, the healing of broken identities and the restoration of voice and purpose.

In the book of Ruth, we see redemption and transformation at work through God's covenant people. Note that in the entire story, God never does audibly communicate with Naomi, Ruth, Boaz, or anyone else. God worked through the people. He restored broken identities through His people. In God's family, the vulnerable are remembered and provided for. The foreigner is treated kindly and generously rather than discriminated against. Back home in community, Naomi's identity was restored and she rediscovered her name. Ruth found a new place to call home, a new people to call family. Her new purpose and contribution are highlighted still in David's ancestry.

There is a healing and empowering that God
brings to us through other people. We all need it.

Your circumstances may not call to mind what Ruth and Naomi experienced, but it's vital that you recognize the role of God's family in the transformation of your identity and purpose. Perhaps because relying on the community of faith doesn't seem as "spiritual" as other endeavors, it's easy to underestimate the healing, transformative power at work in community life. Yet as intercultural consultant Marianna Pogosyan has noted: "We need others. For completing the patchwork of our identities, with our singular traits and those that we share with kindred and friends. For the safety they give us to pursue our goals. For the affect and meaning they breathe into our lives."[2]

When God is at work in covenant community, His people live the corporate life they were made for. Living with others restores the broken pieces of our lives and affirms and celebrates our full identity. It gives us the safety of belonging. It holds space for our journey and our stories, including our lament. It listens to and for our voice. It equips and unleashes people into their purpose.

There is a healing and empowering that God brings to us through other people. We all need it.

## RESTORED IN SONG

I didn't know this at the time, but music therapists note that when we recall songs that connect with key events in our lives, the remembering grounds us internally and strengthens our connection with others (such as friends and family). In addition, it strengthens our sense of identity, meaning, and purpose.[3]

Each night on the drive back to my hotel, my soundtrack continued. Music transported me to my childhood. I'd once again be dancing with aunties at parties dressed in stunning traditional Nigerian attire. Their geles (head wraps) were resplendent with color and dared to defy gravity. They would join me on the dance floor for a while and tuck a pound note into my little beret. I could recall the smell and the tastes of the food, so much food. Jollof rice (it's not a Nigerian party if there is no jollof), moi moi, fried plantain, chin-chin, pepper soup, and lots of chicken and other meat. And for reasons no one can explain, Scotch eggs. I hadn't eaten that food, our food, for so long now. I missed it. I missed us.

Back in my hotel room, I realized that the music, the songs, the welcome at the conference, the people from so many cultures and ethnicities, all this had restored something in me. The people and experiences were restoring parts of my identity that had been stripped away in my wilderness. Though no one at the event called me by my family name, Oyeniran, or even Modupe (my Nigerian first name), I heard my full name for the first time in a long time. My name resounded in smiles and hugs, in songs and greetings, in a sanctuary filled with a community of women. I realized in the healing that there was a place for all of me in the United States.

The next day in worship, I heard the distinctly African voices, the inflections and accents rising above the others as we sang,

> Our scars are a sign of grace in our lives,
>     And Father how you brought us through.[4]

Tears ran down my cheeks as I thought of the struggles they had faced. Maybe similar to the challenges that my family faced years ago as they rooted themselves in England. They too had gone through the wilderness. They knew what it truly costs for an immigrant *to get the job done.*[5] Yet their song testified to me that God still redeemed the most tender and overlooked parts of our stories. He made them fruitful men and women, who by His grace and power significantly contributed to society while paving a way for those who came after them.

God didn't speak directly to me, yet He spoke so much to me through His people that weekend. I heard God's voice in God's people speaking directly to me. While the songs reminded me that He had brought me through every stage of my life, the people reminded me that God had carried me through the wilderness and given me new life in the valley. He brought me to a place of healing that overshadowed the hurt. He provided security that was stronger than survival and scarcity. It was a remembrance and a reset, and it gave me courage. Yes, I was ready to follow Him into the Promised Land after all.

Finally, I took a deep breath and willed my tears to stop. Not because I was feeling tough, but because Sade had just done my makeup and I didn't want to ruin it. I was about to be introduced to the Sunday morning congregation, and I didn't want to greet these beautiful people looking like a weeping, sniveling hot mess with my makeup on my chin. Been there, done that. I wasn't nostalgic for every part of my history.

My experience that weekend captured what God does when He redeems our stories through life in community.

- He reconnects us to others who remind us of our story.
- He recovers our full name.
- He resets and restores our purpose.

I'll forever be grateful for that powerful God-encounter experienced in community that weekend, but I'm aware that the everyday work of community transformation takes place among the people I live with. My family and my friends, the people I work with, my church community.

## REMEMBER YOUR FULL NAME

After leaving her adopted land of Moab, Naomi needed an environment that would not only comfort her but also bring her a renewed understanding of God and His dealings with His people. She had left Bethlehem during a famine and felt God brought misfortune on her in Moab (see Ruth 1:1, 21). But after being widowed and then made childless, she returned to a place that would protect and provide for her and Ruth both (see Ruth 2). Her understanding of God was transformed with hope once she was back in her home community.

Thankfully no one seemed to pay attention to Naomi's request for a name change. At the end of the story, her community still called her Naomi and celebrated with her, blessing the changes in her life and encouraging more change (see Ruth 4:14–17).

While our personal devotional practices play a huge role in establishing our identity, God provides people to help us. Sometimes they're further along in the journey, and they've seen more. Their identity has been rebuilt in profound ways, and they're happy to share their tools as you rebuild your identity and reclaim your true name. They'll celebrate resurrection of your name over the things that have falsely renamed you, and they'll keep encouraging you.

They are your friends, or perhaps they are mentors. Have you found them?

Many of the battles for my identity were won at a kitchen table over coffee with a mentor. Others were won over a meal with close friends. They called me by my full name, not the things that had wrongly renamed me. They stayed with me even as I stumbled. And when I did stumble, they would keep calling out my full name, keep urging me forward, celebrating every trace of redemption in my life. Sometimes they could see more clearly than I could. They'd talk with me and pray with me until I saw it too.

At times, you might need to seek out resources beyond close friends and mentors. You might need support groups as you journey through grief. You might need groups to help you in recovery as you confront addictions or eating disorders. You might need to spend time with a counselor, someone specifically trained to meet you where you are and help you move forward. Some people might feel embarrassed about the idea of seeing a counselor, as though it's a sign of weakness or a failure of faith. I disagree. We have no problem going to a doctor for a broken leg. Why should we have a problem getting professional help for a broken identity or deeper psychological and emotional challenges? Why wouldn't that be God's provision for you in the same way a general physician is? Don't allow shame or embarrassment to steal your redemption story. I'd rather spend a year in counseling than need it for the next ten. If time with a counselor or therapist will provide the extra support you need, then go for it.

- Who are the people in your life, the closest friends and mentors, who are further ahead and can help you find the way?
- Who is mentoring you through this journey?
- Where do you need qualified, professional support? What are your next steps to find the support you need?

It has been said that "a friend is someone who knows the song in your heart and can sing it back to you when you have forgotten the words."[6] Who are the people in your life who can sing your song back to you?

For me, it's my husband who advocates for me and encourages me to dream bigger. It's my closest friends who remind me of dreams I tend to shelve when life gets out of control. In such times, they whisper my dreams back to life. For you, it might be people who don't know you well but, while watching you in action, see something that connects with your purpose. They see what is there and they encourage you.

> While our personal devotional practices
> play a huge role in establishing our
> identity, God provides people to help us.

When you lose your voice, you certainly need someone who knows you well enough to know the song in your heart and remind you of what you're living for. Remember, your voice, your vocation, is the expression of your redeemed identity. It needs to be heard. It's a story that needs to be told.

Finally, the great thing about this community is that you are part of it. That means you aren't just a recipient of the blessings of God's family. You're a contributor. You get to reconnect people to the bigger picture when you tell them your story. You will help others recover their names, their full names. You will use your voice to sing the songs they have hidden in their hearts out of fear, and you will help them find their voices and unleash their purpose. This is part of the life *you* were made for.

Are you ready?

# Practices

HEY, SOUL SISTER,

Whenever I'm preparing for a trip, be it a work trip or family adventure, I'm a committed list maker. I'm not always the best at *completing* the list, but I love a good list nonetheless. In fact, I'm so committed to them that I even add a few already completed tasks, just for the sheer joy of crossing them out and feeling accomplishment!

When I'm packing for a trip to visit our families overseas, I don't want us to be panicking about where our passports are after we've already arrived at the airport. I need to know in advance where all the essentials are packed and that the most-needed items are easily accessible. There is security in checking things off the list.

Like a long trip toward a desired destination, your journey of identity and purpose will continue long after you've finished reading this book. Believe me when I tell you an adventure awaits! Naturally, you'll feel that you should be prepared. It's tempting to compile a list of tasks, possibly even with a time-table in mind. I'll nail down my struggle with insecurity by month's end, then I'll get serious about working on my perfectionism.

While it might seem that making a list will reduce the likelihood of surprises along the way, remember that you don't possess God's ability to see the future. Only God understands the timetable for bringing transformation to the deepest caverns of your heart.

On the other hand, it would be disingenuous to say you don't need to do anything, as though you can simply wish yourself into freedom and purpose. You have an active relationship with God, not a passive one, right? It's the same with furthering your journey of identity and purpose.

As much as I love having a list when I travel, I'd like to propose an alternate approach for your journey of identity and purpose. As you go forward, make room for God to meet with you. Look at the life you have with all its demands and commitments. Develop realistic habits, create viable spaces in your schedule, commit to simple (doable!) practices that give God regular access to your heart and mind.

Make room in your life for God to do the work in shaping you into who you were created to be. With that in mind, in this chapter I'll offer nothing more than a few suggestions that I hope will inspire your own ideas as you make room for God.

If you decide to call it your Making-Room-for-God List, I understand. Some old habits die hard, and you've got to organize your ideas somehow. Just don't color-code it, okay?

Keep making space,

Jo

ᘓ

"Honey, it's 6 a.m.," I groaned. As an early riser, it wasn't the time as much as it was the sound. The sound was the problem. At 6 a.m., my youngest daughter was downstairs practicing for her recorder concert. It wasn't how I hoped to start the day. Ever.

"Mom, I need to practice. Come and listen," my ten-year-old said. She worked on re-creating the theme from *Star Wars* on the recorder. I took a deep breath and put the kettle on. This situation required a large, strong cup of herbal tea. I sat there listening, reminding myself that my husband and I have sought to cultivate hard work and persistence in our girls. *This is good,* I told myself. Really it is.

"I'll play it through one more time."

I shook my head. "You don't have to. You've been practicing after school for weeks."

"No, I will. The concert is tomorrow. I need to keep on practicing."

She continued for another fifteen minutes. *You encouraged this,* I thought. *You have only yourself to blame.* I smiled weakly at my girl and took another gulp of tea.

The following day a group of animated fourth graders gathered in the school gym, ready to play their hearts out to their audience of parents. Practice didn't make perfect. (The fourth graders are gorgeous, but no offense—this is the *recorder,* folks!) But even without perfection, it turned out they were very good, and the *Star Wars* theme was a standout.

I noticed something else that night. The kids were giggling and supporting each other, giving each other knowing looks and high fives, having the time of their fourth-grade lives. Practice not only transformed their skills but also transformed them. Practice created shared passion, connection, and fun.

The morning after the concert, my daughter was up early playing the recorder. "Hey," I told her, "I thought you were done. Your concert was yesterday!"

"I know, Mom, but now I'm playing because I just love it!"

Kettle. Tea. She also signed up to learn how to play the saxophone.

As a family, we're in that phase of life where all we seem to do is chauffeur our girls to practices. Sports, music, theater. It's great to watch them improve in something they love or discover a new talent. They love practices, in part because they enjoy sports and competing; and they love music and performing. But the practices also have created and strengthened friendships. They enjoy the way practices spin off into playdates and adventures, a late-night run to grab frozen yogurt after the game, an unexpected movie trip, a sleepover to celebrate the end of a tournament, exchanging numbers with the new kid they met at band practice, the kid who eventually becomes a best friend. And all these memories, relationships, and fun began with practices. For my girls and their fabulous friends, practicing hasn't just developed their skills, it has fueled their passions and shaped their lives.

## Why You Need to Practice

We've seen that our relationship with God is all about transformation. Because of the life, death, and resurrection of Jesus, we are made new. In Him our broken identities fall away. Our old name is exchanged for our new name. We have a new voice and purpose. From its earliest beginnings recorded in the book of Acts through to the present day, the church has adopted practices such as prayer, Bible study, worship, and service to meet with God. Christians want to make space for a transformation that only He can bring.

As we keep embracing God's dream for our lives, we'll need to adopt some practices. As we do that, it's vital we understand why. We don't adopt practices to prove ourselves or to perform for God's approval. We already are seen, known, and loved.

Are you ready to put up your sails and
allow God to continually breathe life
into the Dream of You, redeeming your
identity and restoring your voice?

Instead, the practices make room in our overscheduled lives for God to meet with us. We find that by making time for God's engagement with us, we are changed, transformed, redeemed. And, like the eager fourth-grade recorder players, our practices are an investment in forging friendships and shared experiences. They fuel our passions and sometimes make us giggle together. Practices lead to spontaneous, adventurous moments with God that you didn't see coming. John Ortberg has written, "Our task is to use these activities to create opportunities for God to work. Then what happens is up to him. We just put up the sails: 'The wind blows wherever it chooses.'"[1]

Are you ready to put up your sails and allow God to continually breathe life into the Dream of You, redeeming your identity and restoring your voice? Let's explore some ways we can make room for God to meet with us in our everyday lives. Feel free to add your own practices to the list.

## RECEIVE HOLY COMMUNION AND REMEMBER WHO YOU ARE

On the night when he was betrayed, the Lord Jesus took some bread and gave thanks to God for it. Then he broke it in pieces and said, "This is my body, which is given for you. Do this to remember me." In the same way, he took the cup of wine after supper, saying, "This cup is the new covenant between God and his people—an agreement confirmed with my blood. Do this to remember me as often as you drink it." (1 Corinthians 11:23–25)

When Jesus shared a last supper with His closest friends, they had no idea that within hours life would change for eternity. Jesus would be betrayed three times by one of the twelve. All but one of the others would run away and, in their own ways, deny Jesus in His time of greatest need. Only one would stand at the foot of His cross along with the women who had followed Jesus. They had no idea that some of them would find His tomb empty and that Jesus's death and resurrection would redefine history for all time.

But Jesus knew, so He spent the evening preparing them. He wanted them to be prepared not just for the days ahead but also for the years to come as they formed the first church and spread His good news. One of the ways He prepared them was with a meal that would help them to remember. He used bread and wine. He called the bread His body, the wine His blood. And He said, "Do this to remember me."

Sometimes we remember to look backward, to list events, to recall what happened. Sometimes we remember with nostalgia, recalling the way we felt in that moment, reliving the past. It's inevitable that the disciples would have done this many times after that weekend. Yet Jesus spoke to something deeper, something that would remain relevant for the disciples for the rest of their lives. The same things are relevant to our lives.

Jesus spoke to something that was captured in the *anamnesis*. That word refers to a type of active remembering. It calls the past to mind, not for nostalgia's sake but as a signpost that leads us into the future. It is a memory that speaks to who we are. The English word *amnesia*—"memory loss"—comes from the same Greek root. When we lose our memory, we often lose something of who we are, our identity.

As Jesus prepared His disciples, He called them as well as us to a practice of active remembrance. To actively remember what His broken body means for us, what His shed blood means for us. To actively remember *whose* we are now as we keep in mind who we are now. He invites us to actively remember our identities in the transformative light of redemption, knowing that it defines us as we walk into the future.

> At the Lord's table, I surrender the hurts and hang-ups, the failed coping mechanisms that point to my striving. It's where I confess sin, exchanging my old life for new. I remember all that Jesus has done for me.

Understanding this truth has enriched my experience of communion. For me, communion is an act of giving thanks, of seeking forgiveness and wiping the slate clean. That always has been powerful, this significant practice in which I remember my covenant relationship with God.

In a world that ties my identity to *oughts* and *shoulds,* the practice of receiving holy communion is an active reset of my God-given, Cross-won identity. At the Lord's table, I surrender the hurts and hang-ups, the failed coping mechanisms that point to my striving. It's where I confess sin, exchanging my old life for new. I remember all that Jesus has done for me. I remember again whose I am and what it means for who I am and how I live.

- Do you make a practice of receiving holy communion? What does it mean to you?
- Every time you come to the Lord's table, invite the

Lord to help you remember who you are and whose
you are.

## ALLOW GOD'S WORD TO RENEW YOUR THINKING

And so, dear brothers and sisters, I plead with you to give
your bodies to God because of all he has done for you. Let
them be a living and holy sacrifice—the kind he will find
acceptable. This is truly the way to worship him. Don't
copy the behavior and customs of this world, but let God
transform you into a new person by changing the way you
think. Then you will learn to know God's will for you,
which is good and pleasing and perfect. (Romans 12:1–2)

I was applying the finishing touches to my makeup before I spoke
at an event when I heard, clearly, "Psalm 139. Out loud."

Sensing the Lord's prompting, I found my Bible and read the
psalm out loud in front of a full-length mirror. I'm no longer the
little girl with red boots who dreamed of becoming Wonder
Woman. Though I love gold wristbands and intend to buy another pair of red boots one day. Nor am I the teenager who struggled to be satisfied when she stood in front of a mirror. My
covenant Partner fought for me and won. That said, I have a different body now. It's a little worn and weathered, rounder and
softer in certain spaces. There's more of me to call my own!

I'm the woman who laughs at the unrealistic expectations of
a culture obsessed with youth, but occasionally prays for a faster

metabolism and gets a little bit enamored of the latest health fad. And occasionally I hold in my stomach because . . . well, posture or something.

I've experienced deep healing but remain acutely aware that my body and beauty do not align with the values and optics of Western popular culture. Some days it still takes energy to ignore it all. And courage to remind myself that a woman who looks like me, who knows her identity and owns her voice, may never make the cover of an airport-newsstand magazine but still is fearfully and wonderfully made in the image of God.

When I finished reading the text, I stood in front of the full-length mirror and thought about how far I'd come and where I still had room to grow and heal. I didn't have to lift my head; it was already lifted. That's how I hold my head most days.

*I praise You that my eyes and my teeth are fearfully and wonderfully made. Thanks for my mouth and my nose and my smile, even for these tiny cute ears.*

*I thank You and I praise You for my black skin. I was always right about that one; You were always right about that one.*

*I thank You for these arms, strong enough to hold the people I love. I thank You for my hands that You've put to work to create, to enjoy.*

Then I laid a hand on my stomach and sighed deeply. Fondly. I looked down at my midsection.

*I thank You, Lord, for my fearfully and wonderfully made stomach. It never did flatten, did it? My abs lie deep, deep within! But this part of my body carried two girls and brought them to me. And the added stretch marks that joined the others are the marks of my mothering, and I'm so proud of my daughters, so grateful that I got to become a mom. So, thank You, Lord.*

*(That said, Lord, if You ever want me to rediscover where my abs are, I want You to know that I too am open to that. I also thank You for the woman who made Spanx and I pray You bless her richly.)*

*I praise You, Father, that my feet are fearfully and wonderfully made. They're a bit arthritic in my toes now, and I realize I took them for granted. I thank You also for that time when, after my feet grew another size after having my first child (didn't see that warning in the pregnancy books!), You heard my sincere prayers for that not to happen after my second. I'm also grateful for Nordstrom Rack.*

I sighed again and smiled as God met with me in His Word all over again. I'm a work in progress, but I'm so happy with the progress.

The Bible describes itself as living and active. Are we making room for God's Word to live and act in our lives? Seek God and search for verses, chapters, and passages that speak His perspective on your identity, your voice, your body, the giants you battle against, and the other battles that none of us can avoid. Read His words aloud, inviting God to connect these words of truth to your core and to rewire your thinking patterns. Read them throughout your day.

> As you move forward, renew your mind
> with God's life-giving, stronghold-
> slicing, truth-telling words.

I promise you this exercise will feel like an exercise; it won't feel sexy and hip. You'll likely feel exhausted and completely out of shape! But over time, almost imperceptibly at first, you'll get fitter, feel stronger, and be healthier. Don't stop. In a while you will look back and see how far you've come. As you move forward, renew your mind with God's life-giving, stronghold-slicing, truth-telling words.

- How can you make room in your life for God to meet you with His life-giving words?
- What will you put on hold or set aside in order to make sure this happens?

## Ask God to Breathe New Life into You

Don't act thoughtlessly, but understand what the Lord wants you to do. Don't be drunk with wine, because that will ruin your life. Instead, be filled with the Holy Spirit, singing psalms and hymns and spiritual songs among yourselves, and making music to the Lord in your hearts. (Ephesians 5:17–19)

As Paul taught and trained the Christian community in Ephesus to keep moving in their relationship with God, he urged them to be filled with the Spirit. "Instead," he wrote to them, "be filled with the Holy Spirit." Be filled and *go on being filled.* Refill and repeat.

The Holy Spirit is not an extra or a denominational preference; the Holy Spirit is a Person of the Trinity. The Spirit was present at creation (see Genesis 1). It was the Spirit who entered Ezekiel's valley of dry bones and so transformed the lifeless bones that they eventually stood to their feet as an army (see Ezekiel 37).

Jesus was filled with the Spirit and empowered by the Spirit in ministry (see Luke 4). He told His disciples that they would be empowered by the Holy Spirit just as He was (see John 14–16; Acts 1). The word Jesus used to describe the Holy Spirit, *Paraclete,* refers in the Greek to one who comes alongside. It's a word that is translated as Helper, Advocate, Comforter, Counselor. The Spirit comes alongside us to convict us of sin, while leading us into truth. The New Testament teaches that the same Spirit that raised Christ from the dead lives in us (see Romans 6; 8), produces fruit in our lives, and empowers us with gifts. Let's make space for the Holy Spirit to continually fill and transform our lives.

Years ago when I attended a Sunday-evening service in hopes of impressing the worship-band drummer, the Holy Spirit spoke to some in the congregation. He let them know a girl in the congregation had never understood the Father's love. The couple who listened to me afterward and talked with me were able to reveal the fruit of the Spirit in abundance. The tangible peace that enveloped me was the Paraclete at work, comforting me and making me new.

Inviting the Holy Spirit to move in power is a prayer that the earliest church prayed. The regular practice of inviting the Holy Spirit to fill me is essential for a recovering overachiever such as I am. It reminds me that I am not transformed by my striving or proving. I am transformed by the power of God.

- When was the last time you asked God to fill you with His Spirit?
- What do you do to practice making room for the presence and work of the Holy Spirit in your life?

## MEETING GOD IN PRAYER

Keep on asking, and you will receive what you ask for.
Keep on seeking, and you will find. Keep on knocking,
and the door will be opened to you. For everyone who
asks, receives. Everyone who seeks, finds. And to everyone
who knocks, the door will be opened. (Matthew 7:7–8)

I was stuck. Years after God had revealed Himself to me as Father, I hit another unexpected roadblock. I began grieving my father's absence again—this time in a completely different way than I had in my younger years. I'd see my friends' fathers pick them up from college for Christmas break or at the end of the spring semester. Or I'd see a dad helping his daughter make a move into a new house. I'd hear them giving great car advice. It hurt more deeply than I was prepared for.

On the day I graduated from college, I expected to be sad. But

I wasn't, because my mom and Aunty Bassey were hilarious company that day. I expected to feel a tender pang on my wedding day, but my two brothers gave me away and it was perfect. On the days of big occasions, I had people who loved me well.

It was on ordinary days, when I noticed people doing routine things, that my dad's absence pierced my heart and soul. I never expected that my heart would break and my eyes would fill up every time a friend's dad carried boxes of books in from the car, helping her move into an apartment!

Thank God for practices I had put into place. My patterns of prayer helped me get unstuck. My prayer life took on a level of raw honesty so that I could freely express my anger, confusion, and disappointment. One night, after lying in bed and talking with God until dawn, I got up to face the day knowing two things:

1. I needed caffeine.
2. Something had shifted in my relationship with God.

My patterns of prayer have created space for confession, thanksgiving, asking, seeking, and knocking. They also have created space for listening. Prayer is my place of no pretense, just sitting down to talk with my Father about life, love, and everything else. Talking as though we've got all night. And sometimes, we do have all night.

Your heavenly Father is listening
to you. Ask. Seek. Knock.

It sounds too obvious to mention, but prayer is key for our journey. I'm not going to tell you to get rid of your prayer lists because, as you know, I'm a fan of lists. And while I never fully stick to them, I pray a lot more when I have a list than when I don't. But I encourage you to make room in your prayer life for all God wants to do in you. Don't forget to pray for yourself while you're busy praying for everyone else. Don't forget to ask Him to transform you. Ask Him to redeem your identity and lead you to the life you were made for.

Your heavenly Father is listening to you. Ask. Seek. Knock.

- Reflect on your prayer life. Is it a place of honesty and vulnerability?
- How would you like it to grow?

There are many other ways you can make room for God to work in your heart. You might connect with God most profoundly when you're outdoors enjoying nature. Or in times of worship, when you are singing, filled with music and praise. Perhaps even in solitude and silence. The main thing is that you develop practices that empower you to make room for God. He will meet you there.

## GOOD GIFTS FROM A GOOD GOD

You parents—if your children ask for a loaf of bread, do you give them a stone instead? Or if they ask for a fish, do you give them a snake? Of course not! So if you sinful people know how to give good gifts to your children, how much more will your heavenly Father give good gifts to those who ask him. (Matthew 7:9–11)

A few years ago, someone reached out to my brother and me on Facebook, asking if we knew Aunty May. It had been thirty years, but I recognized the person immediately. This was Adrian, one of our neighborhood friends, part of a big group who played together all the time. Adrian had searched for us over the years, wondering what had become of us. He didn't know we'd both left England.

This marked the first time it occurred to me that when we left Aunty May, our friends had missed us. We eagerly filled each other in on the past thirty years. Then Adrian shared some pictures of our childhood posse. Every photograph told a story: the gang playing together, eating popsicles, summer vacation, posing like we were superheroes. Our neighborhood adventures.

I realized that every photograph told *my* story—who I was, how happy I was. I'd forgotten how happy I had been as a young child. I'd been defined by a wintery December day that buried my stories in sorrow and loss. I'd lost my happy memories and a piece of my identity. This moment returned the happiness of childhood to me as I looked at the old neighborhood photos. I had asked the Lord to redeem my life, and this was one of the beautiful ways that He answered. This redemptive reconnection to the past grounded me and gave me a new signpost toward the future. I didn't know I needed this gift until I received it. I knew it was yet another expression of God's redeeming love.

- What unexpected gifts have surfaced in your life and redeemed a piece of your identity?

ꮯꮲ

We all know that practicing is not always exciting or glamorous. It is practical not pretty, and it requires dedication and work. But your practices will create space for a closer connection with God that will transform you and ground your identity. They'll make room for shared experiences with Him that restore your voice. They'll open the door to unexpected moments that you welcome once they appear. Like my joyful daughter after an elementary-school recorder concert, you'll find yourself practicing more, just for the love of it.

# Pick Up Your Keys

As I mentioned earlier, when I was a child, about four years old, I wanted to be Wonder Woman when I grew up. My naive, imperfect dream developed through wounded filters and a broken worldview. So my innocent dream deteriorated into over-achieving and proving I was of value.

I didn't know my name, and I'd long before lost my voice. But as I wrote at the beginning of this book, there is something important about our unfiltered, innocent dreams. Because even with their imperfections, our early dreams give us signposts to our aspirations and ideals. They might even hint at the kind of life we were made for.

I wanted to be Wonder Woman because she was empowered to change the world for good. I wanted to be Wonder Woman because she wasn't just all talk; Wonder Woman got things *done*. It wasn't about her fame or popularity, it was about her impact and influence. She helped people; she rescued people. She changed the world and made it better for people to live in. *That meant something.*

I wanted to be part of a big adventure, the kind that was bigger than me, the kind that meant something and changed the world for good. Even as a little girl, I knew, *I just knew,* that that was the life I was made for.

What I didn't know yet was that the opportunity was already out there. But I found out.

## KEYS TO THE KINGDOM

After three days of powerful ministry in the mountains surrounding the Sea of Galilee, where multitudes of people had been healed and four thousand families had been miraculously fed in one sitting, Jesus moved on with his disciples to the region of Caesarea Philippi. It wasn't the type of environment that a first-century Jew would automatically have thought of when seeking rest and retreat.

Twenty-five miles north of Galilee, Caesarea Philippi was a place surrounded by pagan temples where sex rites and other rituals were part of the worship. In its day, it was considered a sin city that represented all that was base and depraved. The city sat at the foot of Mount Hermon, known as the Rock of the Gods due to the shrines built there. At the center of the Rock of the Gods was a cave that was noted as a source of the Jordan River. It was the place where sacrifices were performed. It was known as the gates of hell.

Once there, Jesus asked His disciples about who the community thought He was. When the disciples responded with a variety of answers, He asked a more personal question: "But who do you say I am?" (Matthew 16:15).

Jesus did not need the affirmation of His followers. Rather, He was asking them to engage with Him in the midst of a place that was ugly and broken. They had been walking through communities where sin reigned and people were exploited. In the middle of suffering and false gods, Jesus wanted His followers to think about who He was.

> Simon Peter answered, "You are the Messiah, the Son of
> the living God."
> Jesus replied, "You are blessed, Simon son of John,
> because my Father in heaven has revealed this to you. You
> did not learn this from any human being. Now I say to
> you that you are Peter (which means 'rock'), and upon this
> rock I will build my church, and all the powers of hell will
> not conquer it. And I will give you the keys of the King-
> dom of Heaven. Whatever you forbid on earth will be
> forbidden in heaven, and whatever you permit on earth
> will be permitted in heaven." (Matthew 16:16–19)

Simon received a revelation from the Father, and it connected! He recognized that Jesus was the Messiah, the One his people had been waiting for. Jesus was the One God had sent to change the course of history, to rescue people from oppression and sin. Jesus was and is *it*. He was the good news, the Son of the living God. In what we now know was a transforming covenant moment, Jesus gave Simon a new name and with it a new identity. Starting at that moment, he was Peter—no longer named by his past and limited by where he had been. Now renamed by God, Peter's character, his personality, and his call were redefined.

Whoever you are, wherever you've been, God can transform your identity. You might be hungry and broken by life. You might feel like you're living in the original sin city. You might be living just outside the gates of hell. Jesus sees you, and He can reach you and redeem you. He will give you a new name, mightier than everything that has named you in the past. It's in Christ that we find out who we are.

Peter's new name would be amazing enough, but Jesus didn't stop there. He made it clear that through Peter He would build the church. Even the gates of hell couldn't overcome the movement of passionate believers that was to come.

Then Jesus gave Peter a set of keys. "And I will give you the keys of the Kingdom of Heaven. Whatever you forbid on earth will be forbidden in heaven, and whatever you permit on earth will be permitted in heaven" (Matthew 16:19).

In the Bible, keys are always a symbol of authority. Peter now had the authority of the kingdom of heaven. This kingdom did not refer to a geographical area. Rather, the word for kingdom—*basileia*—refers to the kingship of God, God's rule in a place or situation.

What was Peter being given? What does the kingdom of heaven look like? It looks like what happened when Jesus walked and moved in conversations with people and in communities of people. It looks like what happens when heaven touches earth. It looks like good news: forgiveness, mercy, healing, love, justice, and restoration.

When heaven touched earth, people were set free from the kingdom of darkness. The former untouchables were touched, the outcasts were given a place in the community, the people who had been singled out for hate were radically loved, and the people who were far from God and who tried for years to be good enough to be loved discovered that God loved them. The kingdom of heaven looked exactly like proclamation, the message of salvation and freedom.

> What does the kingdom of heaven look like?
> It looks like what happened when Jesus
> walked and moved in conversations with
> people and in communities of people.

In redeeming Peter's identity, Jesus restored His followers' sense of purpose. A new purpose did not stop at believing in Jesus and being personally transformed. Peter's purpose—which was the same as that of every follower of God—was not only to know God but also to represent Him wherever the follower was called by God to live and develop relationships. Now authorized and empowered by Jesus's authority and power, every part of Peter's life became a kingdom opportunity.

## IN CHRIST WE FIND OUT WHAT WE LIVE FOR

It took a while for Peter to grow into his new identity and purpose. Brash and presumptuous, he sometimes got ahead of himself or out of his depth. He would risk something for God and then retreat to personal safety. But in the book of Acts, we read that Peter proclaimed the good news of Jesus Christ, and in one day three thousand people were saved. With that, the church was born.

Peter healed a begging man who had a physical disability. And he did it in the *name* of Jesus. The man, Aeneas, was able to get out of bed for the first time in eight years after Peter spoke the name of Jesus in healing. Peter raised Dorcas back to life. Peter led the fledgling yet growing church community. He shared the good news of life in Christ with Cornelius, a Roman centurion. Then Cornelius and his family were baptized in the name of Jesus.

When we look at the first-century church, we see transformed believers living in kingdom purpose in every part of their lives.

Stephen, the first Christian martyr, was a waiter. Paul, Priscilla, and Aquila planted churches, trained leaders, and made tents. Eunice and Lois were mother and grandmother to Timothy and nurtured his faith, producing one of the key leaders of the early church. Luke was a doctor; Lydia was a businesswoman. Still their lives overflowed with purpose. A home was not just a home, a meal was more than a meal, a job more than a job. All of life presented opportunities to see God's kingdom come and His will be done in their little piece of earth as it was in heaven.

The good news they had discovered was far too important to keep to themselves. So heaven's healing and freedom, justice and mercy, forgiveness and power, not to mention grace and love, touched a scorched earth through ordinary men and women transformed by Jesus. Ministry happened in everyday life.

## Life at Home with a New Name

In my house there is a mirror and a little table near my front door. That's where we often put our keys. The idea behind it is that I briefly check myself in the mirror, pick up my keys, and go out into the world to get on with the day. It doesn't always work that way.

Some days I get a little . . . preoccupied with myself in the mirror. There are days when I am especially pleased with how together I'm looking. I look fantastic! Then there are days I'm not as impressed with what I've thrown together. There are other days that, frankly, I look ridiculous, so I burst out laughing. When I'm distracted, I forget that I'm actually going somewhere and need to get my keys. Other days I can't even find my keys, and it's certain that I'm not going anywhere until I find them.

It's important to take a good long look in the mirror, as it were, to see who you really are, to see what's out of place, what needs rearranging. But let's remember the end goal is not purely that we like what we see in the mirror. It's easy to become preoccupied, wondering if we're enough or too much. It's as though we stand in front of the mirror wondering, *Do my spiritual gifts look big in this? Do I need some spiritual Spanx to rein me in?*

Don't get me wrong. There are times we need the long look in the mirror; we need to see what God sees and invite Him to work on our identity. It's redeeming, transformative, and empowering. It's simply that God still has more for us.

A healthy identity opens our life to abundant purpose. As God has redeemed the broken pieces of my life, I find there is more room for all that He brings. There is greater capacity to go where He sends me, to respond to His call.

There is less of me—of my self-absorption and self-protection—and there is more room for others. There's less energy spent striving and proving and more room for dreaming. When I'm not investing my energy in what I think I should be according to the standards of others, I am free to run into all that I actually am. I can unwrap the gifts God has given me and do it without shame or anxiety. I can deploy my skills and gifts and passions in His service without wondering if I am okay. I *am* okay; I'm His child. I'm free to learn and fail and grow. Yes, I'm a work in progress, but I'm making progress. It shows in less of me and more of Him.

I used to be afraid of it, but now I am discovering the depths and height and breadth of God's redeeming, transforming love. I want Him to redeem every fiber of my body, mind, and soul, as well as every second of my life. I want that kind of redemption for me and for the world around me. That's why I have chosen to be a lifelong learner, a disciple of Jesus, rather than wear myself out trying to achieve goals shaped by a broken past or by popular culture. Instead of being a perfectionist, I'll be a follower of the One who really changed the world for eternity.

We are inspired when we read about Simon being given the name Peter and, along with his new name, being commissioned and called in a new way. How could anyone read that account and not be uplifted and inspired? But now you and I have our own stories of redemption, transformation, and calling. We're being transformed from the inside out, and it is changing our lives.

We've got security, peace, and wholeness. It's what others are searching for and the kind of good news that's too good to keep to ourselves. It's time to be *bold*.

You have purpose: you can play your part in bringing the kingdom of heaven to the scorched places of your family, your community, your workplace, your city, and your world. It's time to act.

> When I'm not investing my energy in what I
> think I should be according to the standards of
> others, I am free to run into all that I actually am.

Consider these women:

Vicky is a grandmother who in her spare time is engaged in the fight against human trafficking. She helps rescue young women, setting them on the road to recovery and freedom.

Tiffany speaks words of love to women in a local strip club. She tells them they are seen, known, and fearfully and wonderfully made. She is there every month. They don't hear words like that very often.

Bernadette is a single woman who fosters babies until their parents have rebuilt their lives.

Sharon hosts her neighbors for a weekly meal and get-together that brings connection and joy to the community.

Jen leads the moms-and-preschoolers group in the area.

Caren is a pastor of her church.

Amy is a teacher.

Eva is a barista.

Kim is a church planter who trains new leaders.

Amanda is an artist for the glory of God.

Grace homeschools her children.

Sarah is a successful entrepreneur, looking to empower her staff and build a great company.

Jamie is a single woman helping refugees get settled into quality housing as they rebuild their lives.

They are different women who vary by age, ethnicity, and marital status. Some have children; some do not. Yet they share a single trait: they are actively living into their God-given purpose and using their voices to make a significant difference in the world. They don't do it in their own strength; they recognize that because of whose they are they have kingdom power and authority. They rely on and follow Him. What an adventure!

You have permission to live into your purpose. You were commissioned to do this a long time ago (see Matthew 28:18–20). But have you got directions for your purpose, and have you got your keys?

## WAYS TO BEGIN LIVING INTO YOUR PURPOSE

Here are a few suggestions that will help activate your imagination and get you moving.

### Storyboard to find out what your story is.

Write things down: ideas, plans, dreams, next steps, the things you have to offer others.

Paint, draw, sketch, design. Create and craft your faith journey. Include where you were before Jesus redeemed your identity, what the brokenness looked like. Depict as well how Jesus met you in your brokenness and the changes you're seeing now. Show how they are changing your life.

### Share your journey with others.

Think about who might benefit from hearing how God has changed you already, and how He continues to work in your life. When Jesus sends us out, a key place He sends us to is *the life we already have.* Look around you and notice where you are and whom you are with. Is there someone close at hand with whom you can share what God is doing in your life?

As part of my work, I spend a lot of time on planes. There have been plenty of opportunities to listen and talk to, even pray with, fellow passengers. We start with stories, sometimes very personal stories, but not always. Everyone has a story, and most people want to share theirs. I know that once we're buckled in and off the ground, it's time to put down my book, unplug the headphones, and be available.

Are you available for God to use your story in the lives of others? Pray for opportunities to share your journey with people. Pray that you will recognize them when they come your way, and for the boldness to share when opportunities appear.

Ask God to point out the people He has sent to you, the ones you should pray for and share with. Ask God for the peace to be yourself, to be open to others and to speak what God has given you to say (see Luke 10).

*Sing the song in your heart.*

Take a personal inventory.

- What were the vision and dreams, the voice that was yours, that got bullied into silence?
- What pieces of your purpose were laid aside when you were living under a mistaken identity?
- What are the ideas and plans that you think about, but still feel too inadequate to undertake?
- What is the song in your heart? How can you begin to sing it?

As you take a personal inventory, pray through at least one and write it down. Write down the song in your heart for your family, your neighborhood, your city, and the nations, for your generation. If you've forgotten the words, find the friend who can sing it back to you.

Give yourself permission to dream again. And then dream bigger. What would be a next step for you to take?

It's time to learn from Isaiah's words to God's people and grow into the person who will use her identity to share God's glorious living beyond her own redeemed life.

> They will rebuild the ancient ruins
> and restore the places long devastated. (61:4, NIV)

# Rebuild, Restore, Renew

MY DEAR SISTER,

You didn't think I'd forget to say goodbye, did you?

Here we are, at the end of the beginning of your journey. It's the end of the book, but the work that God has begun in your heart and mind is fresh and new. Signs of resurrection and redemption are budding and beginning to blossom, breaking through the cloak of a long winter. Enjoy it, there's so much more to come.

Still I wanted to speak to the moments ahead that won't feel so luminous. The inevitable periods that will feel weary and tiring and ugly and unbearably old. When you will feel that you are stuck in a long winter. For those moments, I'm reminded of Isaiah's comforting words to God's exiled people, living in a world that didn't reflect who they fully were.

The Spirit of the Sovereign LORD is on me,
    because the LORD has anointed me
    to preach good news to the poor.
He has sent me to bind up the brokenhearted,
    to proclaim freedom for the captives
    and release from darkness for the prisoners,

to proclaim the year of the LORD's favor
    and the day of vengeance of our God,
to comfort all who mourn,
    and provide for those who grieve in Zion—
to bestow on them a crown of beauty
    instead of ashes,
the oil of gladness
    instead of mourning,
and a garment of praise
    instead of a spirit of despair. (Isaiah 61:1–3, NIV)

It was a message of hope and the comfort of God's presence and power when the people were burdened by desperate circumstances. Even in the darkest places, God can turn things around. He brings healing, freedom, deliverance, comfort, and beauty. It's good news! It's no wonder Jesus opened His ministry with some of these words in Luke 4 (see verses 18–19). Then Jesus fulfilled this announcement in His life, death, and resurrection.

Let these words be good news for you. God has not stopped working in you and on you. He is transforming you, making all things new.

By the way, Isaiah was not done with his proclamation from God.

They will be called oaks of righteousness,
    a planting of the LORD
    for the display of his splendor.

They will rebuild the ancient ruins
    and restore the places long devastated;
they will renew the ruined cities
    that have been devastated for generations.
      (Isaiah 61:3–4, NIV)

It's amazing to think that people who are living in exile, broken people, will one day be oaks. They will be strong, mature, liberated people displaying God's splendor through their redeemed identities. And these once-broken ones, these oaks, will rebuild the ruined cities and restore the abandoned places in their ravaged society.

The promise stands for you and me too. When Jesus rescued us, we received good news and freedom, comfort and beauty. Once fragile and broken, now we're like strong oaks displaying His splendor. We show the world a redeemed identity, a full voice, and a new purpose—a new purpose of following behind the Rescuer as part of His rescue team, transforming lives and communities with a message of good news. We are involved with God in making all things new.

Let's not allow a sense of inadequacy to tell us we're not ready or not enough for the task. It would be easy to allow that to happen, because we once were the broken ones who now are sent to serve other broken lives and communities. Maybe we'll remember to be tender and nonjudgmental as we recall our own stories.

Perhaps it's because we know how hard and long we've had to fight and stand to regain our voices that He entrusts us with communities that have been devastated. We know it takes time. We won't be offering a quick fix. We'll be prepared to do the humble, tough work of diligently loving communities back to life. And we have the story of God's power at work in our lives to share. We have God's hope to offer hope wherever we're led to serve.

Healed people can heal people.

Freed people can free people.

Changed people can play their part in seeing lives and communities changed.

Yes, you're ready to share good news. You were seen and loved, and His redemption set you free. He has transformed your identity, He has given you a voice, and He enriches your life with purpose.

Enjoy it. It's the Dream of You.

Jo

# Acknowledgments

It takes a village to write a book, or at least it does for me. So much thanks and love and carbs/healthy snacks are due:

To my loves: my husband, Chris, for telling me to dream bigger and for supporting me every step of the way. I love you, babe. To my gorgeous girls, Tia and Zoë. I am SO proud to be your mom. Thanks for the endless encouragement, snacks, and fun!

To the many, many people who have cheered me on as I've been writing. You've prayed, texted, Voxed, called, sent me treats (yay, Deidra and Libby!), and encouraged me all the way. JHat—I love you, girl. Thanks for being a sister and a friend. Jennie, Amena, Tasha, Vivian, Kathy, Gina, Steph, Sarah, Nish, Bianca, Sal, Rosilyn, Yarbs, Lizzy, Suse, Joy, to name but a few! And Ann, thanks for your beautiful words and your beautiful friendship. You blow me away.

To my community: my friends at Mission Point Church, the Lead Stories Community, my huddles (#mustbehuddle), all the gang at 3DM, and the team who pray for our family.

To my local Starbucks baristas who let me nurse one drink for five hours at a time when writing. And thanks for the free treats! Also to the librarians at my local library, who kindly ignored the amount of food I smuggled in and the loud crunching noises I tried to stifle. Thank you for expanding your definition of silence

To my team:

PA's past and present—Jessie, Steph N., and now Jo. Thank you. You know I'd be lost without you. And incredibly disorganized.

My literary agent and friend, Wendy. You have been a gift at such seminal points in my life. I'm humbled and grateful for the way you've always heard my voice and always encouraged me to use it. Thank you, Wendy, for more than words could say. To Jim, my booking agent, you're amazing. What an adventure it's been working with you! Still: Honey Crisp > Envy. Yeah, I said it. I ain't sorry.

Big love to Shannon (Shanley) Marchese, my editor, to Ron and Pam, and to Kelli for your awesome cover design. To the rest of #TeamWaterBrook for your investment in this project and your friendship and kindness along the way. And to Zakiya. You're all fab, you are.

Finally, to the One who has always seen me, always loved me, and always known my name; the One who restored my voice and gave me purpose. Thank You. I love You.

# Notes

*Introduction: Red Boots*

1. Carol S. Dweck, PhD, *Mindset: The New Psychology of Success* (New York: Ballantine, 2016), 6.

*Chapter 1: Don't Call Me "Pleasant"*

1. Clotaire Rapaille, *The Culture Code: An Ingenious Way to Understand Why People Around the World Live and Buy as They Do* (New York: Broadway, 2006), 58.

2. For more on this, see Craig S. Keener, *Acts: An Exegetical Commentary,* vol. 3, *15:1–23:35* (Grand Rapids: Baker Academic, 2012).

3. For wider reading on covenant, check out Mike Breen, *Covenant and Kingdom: The DNA of the Bible* (Pawleys Island, SC: 3DM Publishing, 2010).

*Chapter 2: What's in a Name?*

1. Found in R. E. Longacre's essay on Joseph in *Dictionary of the Old Testament: Pentateuch,* eds. T. Desmond Alexander and David W. Baker, The IVP Bible Dictionary Series (Downers Grove, IL: IVP, 2003), 476. Walter Brueggemann

has described the coat as a sign of "regal status"; see Brueggemann, *Genesis: Interpretation: A Bible Commentary for Teaching and Preaching* (Atlanta: Westminster John Knox Press, 1986), 300.

### Chapter 3: The Talk

1. Jill Lepore, "The Surprising Origin Story of Wonder Woman," *Smithsonian Magazine,* October 2014, www.smithsonianmag.com/arts-culture/origin -story-wonder-woman-180952710/.

### Chapter 4: The Day I Lost My Voice

1. From the song "Who Will Buy?" from the musical *Oliver!* Music and lyrics by Lionel Bart. Published by Hollis Music, Inc., 1960.

2. The term was coined by clinical psychologists Pauline Clance and Suzanne Imes in 1978 after interviewing a range of top executives. They noted that regardless of the executives' achievements, these women often felt like frauds who were about to be exposed. See for example, Kirsty Walker, "The Imposter Syndrome: Why Women Shouldn't Feel Like Frauds," TedXWhitehall Women talk, Dec. 18, 2013, https://youtu.be/xe9oSV9tZE0.

3. Tom Huddleston, "Lupita Nyong'o: 'If I'm Having a Cinderella Moment, Why Not Enjoy the Hell Out of It?'" September 26, 2016, *Time Out,* www.timeout.com/london /film/lupita-nyongo-if-im-having-a-cinderella-moment-why -not-enjoy-the-hell-out-of-it.

## Chapter 5: God's Child

1. For more on this idea, see Paul J. Achtemeier, Joel B. Green, and Marianne Meye Thompson, *Introducing the New Testament: Its Literature and Theology* (Grand Rapids: Eerdmans, 2001), 425.

## Chapter 6: Known and Loved

1. Susan R. Barry, PhD, "Body Image: What Our Changing Body Image Teaches Us About Our Brains," *Psychology Today,* February 7, 2010, www.psychologytoday.com/blog /eyes-the-brain/201002/body-image.
2. *The Psalms: Introduction, Revised Version with Notes and Index,* ed. Rev. T. Witton Davies (Edinburgh: T. C. & E. C. Jack and 34 Henrietta Street, London W.C. 1906), 326.

## Chapter 7: Slay Your Giants

1. Karen Harrington, *Courage for Beginners* (New York: Little, Brown and Company, 2014).

## Chapter 8: The Wander Years

1. David W. Baker, "Essay: Wilderness, Desert," in *Dictionary of the Old Testament: Pentateuch,* ed. T. Desmond Alexander and David W. Baker, The IVP Bible Dictionary Series, (Downers Grove: IVP, 2003), 893.
2. Baker, "Essay: Wilderness, Desert," 896.

## Chapter 10: Breaking Up with Perfection

1. Alli Worthington, *Breaking Busy: How to Find Peace and*

*Purpose in a World of Crazy* (Grand Rapids: Zondervan, 2016), 22.

2. Tom Wright, *Matthew for Everyone, Part One: Chapters 1–15* (Louisville: Westminster John Knox Press, 2004), 136.

### Chapter 11: The Song in My Heart

1. Brené Brown, *Daring Greatly: How the Courage to Be Vulnerable Transforms the Way We Live, Love, Parent, and Lead* (New York: Avery, 2012), 10–11.

2. Marianna Pogosyan, PhD, "On Belonging: What Is Behind Our Psychological Need to Belong?," *Psychology Today*, April 11, 2017, www.psychologytoday.com/blog/between -cultures /201704/belonging.

3. Cathy Malchiodi, PhD, "Music and Memory: Get Back to Where You Once Belonged," *Psychology Today*, August 13, 2008, www.psychologytoday.com/blog/arts-and -health/200808/music-and-memory-get-back-where-you -once-belonged. Malchiodi's full quote is "Music therapists know that by recalling music memories and associating these memories with significant events, our musical memories provide a veritable life review. In turn, these remembrances provide an internal sense of social support and connect us to others, whether through peer groups, classmates, friends, families, or communities. And triggering recollection of our musical histories reinforces identity, strengthening a sense of self, meaning, and purpose throughout the lifespan."

4. "It Is Well with My Soul," chorus words by Horatio G. Spafford, 1873, music by Philip P. Bliss, 1876. New verses written by Matt Redman and Beth Redman, © 2015 sixsteprecords.

5. Deliberate reference to a line from the musical *Hamilton*.

6. The origin of this quote is hotly contested but often attributed to C. S. Lewis.

### Chapter 12: Practices

1. John Ortberg, *The Life You've Always Wanted: Spiritual Disciplines for Ordinary People* (Grand Rapids: Zondervan, 2002), 52.